A NEW VISION FOR YO

BROCK MORGAN

YOUTH
MINISTRY
2027

FOREWORD BY MARK OESTREICHER

Youth Ministry 2027 asks all the right questions. Could disruption and doubt be gifts of the Spirit that move us (and the youth we work with) beyond our comfortable categories and into a wild and holy trek taking us "further up" and "further in"? Could the desperation so many churches feel about their future and the uncontrolled velocity of our culture be the ants in the pants the church needs to move us beyond a gospel that has been reduced to showing up for meetings and not causing a stir? None of us know what the next ten years hold for youth ministry or for the church, but I'm grateful to have Brock Morgan as a sherpa and cartographer into uncharted territory, in which our students will be our teachers and partners in ministry.

Mark DeVries | @markdevriesYMA
Founder and President, Ministry Architects
Cofounder and Permissionary, Ministry Incubators
Author of *Sustainable Youth Ministry*

Whether you've been working with teenagers for a few weeks or a few decades, *Youth Ministry 2027* will challenge you to embrace the future of youth ministry with vision instead of uncertainty and hope instead of fear.

Elle Campbell | @ellllllllllle
Cofounder, StuffYouCanUse.org
Coauthor of *Creating a Lead Small Culture*

The frenetic pace and seemingly overwhelming task of youth ministry does not often lend itself to stepping away and thinking critically about the calling we stepped into; there is just too much to do. We do what we do full speed ahead. Sure, we tinker with what we do, but most of the time we push forward. Brock holds up a stop sign and invites some deeper reflection. He asks some hard questions and proposes some changes to how we do youth ministry. He is the insider-outsider voice. He is outside your specific ministry but inside your calling. In *Youth Ministry 2027*, Brock casts a new vision of youth ministry going forward. His insights into the church, culture, and teenagers are provocative, instructive, and exciting all at the same time. He not only paints a picture for moving into the future with impactful ministry but delves into the personal life of a youth worker working within the church and how to stay in for the long hall. He also calls out a bit of the rascal in us, which is always a good thing because really if youth workers don't push the envelope for change, who will? I think you will enjoy his writing style that is filled with humor and lots of stories from the world of ministering to kids.

Tic Long | @ticlong
Executive Pastor, Journey Community Church
Former President, Youth Specialties

After finishing this book, I texted Brock and said, "I hate you!" I "hate" Brock because this book is just plain truth. It inspires me to know that people like Brock exist and do ministry the way they do, and that I can keep going, I can press on. As I read it, it began to fill me with hope again and a passion to do youth ministry in a "2027" way. The book was thoroughly engaging and inspiring, and as a youth pastor serving at my present church for 23 years, the book affirms the prophetic calling we have as we serve teenagers. *Youth Ministry 2027* makes me want to keep pressing on. Let's go!

Danny Kwon | @dannykwonphd
Youth Pastor, Yuong Sang Church
Author of *Mission Tripping* and *NEXT: Why Church?* (curriculum)

Youth Ministry 2027 is an important reminder for youth workers that if we want to continue reaching teenagers, both now and in the future, we need to reevaluate our methods but not our mission.

Kenny Campbell | @kennnnnnnnny
Cofounder, StuffYouCanUse.org

One thing I love about Brock Morgan is that he is a student of youth ministry, theology, culture, and more! This book is a marvelous melting pot of the aforementioned. In *Youth Ministry 2027*, Brock tackles the consistent elements of yesterday and today, like character development, individuation, and doubt; but he invites the capital-C "Church" into greater collaboration as we partner with students to creatively form the ministry of tomorrow. They are so many quotable lines in this book, but one of my favorites is a simple one: "Teens are super busy and super hurting, and we have to keep the main thing the main thing." Amen, amen, and amen. So simple, but so lost. I found myself encouraged by how I am practicing youth ministry and challenged to think differently, so I don't hold on too tightly.

Brian Aaby | @brianaaby
Director, YS Search

Youth Ministry 2027
A New Vision for Youth Ministry in this Present Future

By Brock Morgan

Youth Ministry 2027

Copyright © 2017 by Brock Morgan

Publisher: Mark Oestreicher
Managing Editor: Tamara Rice
Cover Design: Adam McLane
Layout: Adam McLane
Creative Director: Didymus

Author's interview with Tim Eldred conducted July 2, 2017. May not be reproduced without author's permission. Essay "Stewarding Momentum" by Troone Marchak included with author's permission. Excerpt from *The Book of Common Prayer* is public domain (for further information contact Church Publishing, Inc.).

ISBN-13: 978-1-942145-35-6
ISBN-10: 1-942145-35-7

The Youth Cartel, LLC
www.theyouthcartel.com
Email: info@theyouthcartel.com
Born in San Diego. Printed in the U.S.A.

CONTENTS

FOREWORD

By Mark Oestreicher

My favorite museum of any kind, anywhere in the world, is
the Tate Modern in London. Housed in the architecturally
repurposed massive shell of a former power plant on the edge
of the River Thames, within eyesight of St. Paul's Cathedral,
the Tate Modern houses, in my opinion, the best collection of
modern art anywhere in the world.

It's the Tate Modern that helped me conclude that Mark
Rothko just might be my favorite artist of all time. His
seemingly simple, deceptively rich palettes of drenched and
vibrant color are mesmerizing and can hold my attention for
extended periods of time. His paintings are the sort that cause
the uninitiated to comment, "Well, even I could paint that"; to
which art critics would respond, "Uh, no you couldn't."

Rothko paintings, like the museum that holds them, aren't
actually *new*, or even particularly *futuristic*. But these paintings
(and the Tate Modern) transport me to a feeling of potential, a
depth of what is possible. They were extremely futuristic when
painted (in the 1950s and 1960s!). Today, they are in no way
a depiction of the future; but they still carry, for me at least, a
feeling of the future.

There's a difference between a prediction of the future and a
vision for the future. This book is the latter, not the former.

Brock's first book with The Youth Cartel—*Youth Ministry in a
Post-Christian World*—was a bit more predictive. But in these
pages, Brock is painting with story and vibe and passion. Brock
isn't interested in a detailed description of what youth ministry
will look like in the year 2027. Instead, he's longing for those
of us who are called to this beautiful work to lean into change,

along with teenagers living in a changing world, in order to see a new movement arise.

One of the best perks of the work I've been blessed to be a part of over the last couple decades is that I get to travel the world, almost always in connection with youth ministries in other countries. I have a major wanderlust compulsion, and I'm a collector of experiences. So I'm particularly blessed to travel to four to six countries each year. My primary learning from these travels is:

Everywhere I go in the world, the best youth ministries are weird. They have a high degree of self-knowledge about their uniqueness, and they celebrate that, even relish in it.

Along these lines, this book is not intended to give you an eight-step plan for re-creating your ministry for future success (really, you should be *extremely* skeptical of any book that makes promises like that—that may have worked in 1982, but those days are long gone). But if you take the time to roll around in these (true) stories from a fellow in-the-trenches youth worker, percolate on his ruminations, and stare deeply into the complex questions he raises, you just might find yourself dreaming of a new movement—involving the teenagers God has placed in your midst—that propels you to risk and hope.

– Mark Oestreicher

For all of those youth workers who are no longer satisfied with the status quo and who are dreaming and praying and longing for more.

THANK YOU

I am so grateful for you, Kelsey and Dancin. My heart is full.
Thank you for your partnership, for dreaming with me, for our
nightly prayer walks, and for always believing. I love you big
time!

To Paul and Carol, my parents. I have no words. I just thank
you from the deepest place in me. Not there, don't be naughty.

To Marko, Adam, and all of The Youth Cartel family, thank you
for your partnership and for continuing to believe in me. I love
how you are instigating change in everything you do, and I'm
super grateful to play a bit of a role in that.

John Yates, I love you big time. Thank you for having a vision
for and continuing to invest in the next generation.

To the youth ministry team at TFCA, I am so glad to be on a
team with people such as yourselves. I count myself as one of
the lucky ones. Thank you for letting me into your gang!

A super big thank you to Tom Wright. Thank you for your
investment in us all.

Tam, thank you for doing such a bang-up job on the edit and
for keeping my ridiculous sense of humor and voice in the MS.
That, I know, was not an easy job! I bet you're even wanting
to edit this thank you. What restraint you have.

A big thank you to OneRepublic, Fitz and the Tantrums, U2,
Pearl Jam, Foo Fighters, HAIM (not Corey), and Switchfoot.
Thanks for inspiring me and for being the soundtrack to this
book.

SO, I'VE GOT TO SET THIS THING UP

"Hey, Brock," he said, "no worries, man. Just ten more years."

"Ten more years until what?" I asked.

"Just ten more till a movement starts. A major shift is coming, brother."

Now, I've always been skeptical of statements like this, but this one really got my attention. So, I asked him to tell me more. He went on to talk about how the United States has always been about twenty years behind the UK when it comes to spiritual shifts, but with the dawn of the Internet age and social media, which has resulted in the flattening of all things, he sees us as just about ten years back now. And a movement has been happening in post-Christian Europe for almost ten years.

"Dude, it's just around the corner, hang in there."

So, when Mark Oestreicher asked me to think about writing another book for The Youth Cartel, I couldn't get this conversation with my UK buddy out of my mind. In fact, it has absolutely gripped me for the better part of a year. "Just ten more years, man."

I've been praying for a movement for over twenty-seven years of youth ministry. And when I say movement, I don't mean an amazing week at camp followed by a slow dwindle back into normalcy. What I mean is that I've been waiting for a time when God does such an amazing work in and through us and our youth that when we come home from camp, our communities are literally never the same. Our workplaces, schools, and (please, God) our churches see mass transformation.

When I wrote *Youth Ministry in a Post-Christian World*, I explained how the US was heading into a period of time when the primary voices and influences would no longer be Christian. I can say that we're in the midst of this right now, without a doubt. But doubt will be a marker of this generation. They're not just going to buy the church's pat answers any longer, which honestly, is a really good thing. But their kind of doubt is not a heel-in-the-ground, unmovable, already-determined kind of doubt. This generation's doubt is a Thomas kind of doubt.

So, I got off the phone with Marko with this idea of a movement—a movement that actually gets launched by this Thomas generation. And something kind of cool happened. I'm not sure if it was luck, mere coincidence, or the very hand of God, but here's what happened.

I thought, "In ten years it will be 2027. Huh, that kind of has a ring to it." Then I thought, "I wonder if the story of Thomas being moved from doubt to faith to a movement, with the guidance of Jesus, is in a Gospel near chapter twenty, verse twenty-seven?" So, with anticipation, I opened my Bible to John 20:27. Here it is:

> *Then he focused his attention on Thomas. "Take your finger and examine my hands. Take your hand and stick it in my side. Don't be unbelieving. Believe."*
> **– John 20:27 (MSG)**

What? Now, I'm not a signs guy, okay. (Yes, I am.) But this one really got my attention right off the bat. So, I've been prayerfully writing ever since.

My guess is that if you're reading this book, it means you and I share the same heart. You love this generation and you've been praying for God to do a new thing. And after a year now of wrestling with this, I can tell you that I'm all in. My belief, in fact, is that it's a big dream of God's.

Now, before we get carried away, this isn't an end times book or a prophetic word kind of book. It's just a call back to the heart of youth ministry. It's a call to wake up to what God is already doing and to just join him—join him in the scary fun, the gripping passion, and the terrifying joy.

Gang, Aslan is on the move.

*Then he focused his attention on Thomas. "Take your finger and examine my hands.
Take your hand and stick it in my side. Don't be unbelieving. Believe."*
– John 20:27 (MSG)

CHAPTER 1
JOHN 20:27: THE THOMAS GENERATION

I'm staring out of my office window watching the parking garage being built for our church's new site. It's been amazing for me to watch the progress of this whole thing. It's really going up quickly now, but initially it was frustratingly slow going, like evolution—subtle and slow shifts where changes were barely noticeable.

The first thing was a tearing away, a digging deep and a removal of all the mess. Then came the thoughtful and strategic laying of a really strong foundation that will support the whole structure. It reminds me of what we do as youth workers when we walk with these folks who are going through this terrible and wonderful thing called adolescence.

Just this morning I was wasting time watching the construction workers when there was a knock on my office door and one of our amazing youth volunteers popped in to talk with me about one of the girls in her tenth-grade small group. She was super concerned about this particular girl who had been subtly and slowly changing over the past few months. This teen had been moving from a simple childlike faith into questioning the whole thing: *Is there a God? How do we know? Is Jesus really him? What about my Muslim friends?*

This very committed volunteer leader came in worried because these questions were now causing doubt among the other girls. It was spreading like a virus. As you know, this can be quite jarring when you're caring for young people going through this shift in their understanding of God and the world.

But here's the thing that we sometimes forget: Every

adolescent goes through a process called *individuation*. It doesn't always look the same or happen at the same time or to the same degree for each teen, but they all must individuate and separate themselves from parents and authority or the cultural norms around them to discover who they really are. The hope is that this happens while they're still in our youth groups versus after they leave and go away to college, so that we can journey with them through this process. So, when the virus of independent thinking and questioning sweeps over a small group, I get excited. "Yes," I think. "We can really get somewhere in the excavation and the stripping away of small thinking, cultural prejudices, and religion and help lay a foundation that will hold their lives up and launch these young people into adulthood as savvy, thoughtful, and dangerous to a small-thinking world."

THE BEAUTIFUL JOURNEY FROM DOUBT TO BELIEF TO MOVEMENT

I remember when I was in tenth grade sitting in youth group. In the middle of the youth pastor's talk, my friend and I got the giggles. We literally started laughing, and we just couldn't stop. What's more, we had no idea what we were even laughing at. I remember biting my tongue really hard, trying to get myself to stop all the nonsense, but to no avail. Eventually one of us burst out with an explosion of laughter as the whole room full of youth and leaders looked at us like we were absolute morons. (And we were, but it was so much fun.)

I love those moments, and I even enjoy them when it's our teens getting the giggles in the middle of my talks. But back then our youth pastor stopped right in the middle of his message and asked us what the deal was. We calmed down, making sure we didn't make eye contact with each other for the rest of his talk for fear the laughter would emerge all over again. But then after youth group he asked to meet with both of us.

Now I remember this like it was yesterday; it's super clear to me. We were standing in the church kitchen, away from everyone; and our youth pastor began to express his disappointment in our behavior when my friend, out of nowhere, interrupted and exclaimed, "Look man, I don't even believe this stuff, and I probably won't even be coming back here anymore."

I was shocked, but my youth pastor seemed to be unfazed. I stood there, absolutely floored that our youth pastor didn't seem upset. But I remember going home that night wondering what I really believed. I wondered if my friend was right, that all this faith stuff was nonsense. His doubt forced me to dig deep to clear away everything, so I could see clearly and find out if there was something, anything worth building my life on. It ended up being the breaking apart of the soil that would eventually lay a foundation for the days and years to come. When my friend told us he was no longer a Christian, it sent me on a personal discovery of truth that has literally continued to this very day. But I remember initially feeling upset about what my friend said. Like I said, I went home that night wondering what the truth really was. The weird thing was that these questions I started having felt like a betrayal to my family and to my church, and so I kept them secret for a few months. It just didn't feel safe to admit them. It felt wrong to question. So, I struggled in isolation until I just couldn't stand it any longer.

One evening, my father and I went for a long ride in the car where I finally blurted it out and confessed all my doubts and questions and my disbelief. The crazy thing was his response. It completely threw me in an unexpected and beautiful way. "Oh good, Brock!" he exclaimed. "I've been waiting for you to begin the digging process. I was wondering when those awesome questions would bubble up to the surface." When he said it, a relief poured over me that felt like the beginning of a long holiday or like the first day of summer vacation. Complete relief.

See, as a child I was a believer. I remember leaving church after hearing those great stories in the Scriptures and feeling so amazed by who Jesus was and what he did. I remember hearing the pastor tell stories of amazing miracles, and I even experienced God personally in very profound ways, even as a little guy. But it was a naïve faith, and now I was growing up and needed to move to a more thoughtful and sophisticated one. Culture is a complex place full of really smart people who have differing perspectives and worldviews, and I needed a deeper understanding, with nuance and complexities and beautiful subtleties and humility that would help me as I headed out into the grown-up world.

However, the truth is that the American church, for the most part, doesn't like questions, especially the loaded ones many youth are asking. Questions make church people feel uncomfortable, uneasy, and afraid that the queries themselves might lead people into a world of doubt and ultimately a rejection of faith. The crazy thing is that these questions they fear are the very thing that can lead youth into a holistic understanding of their faith. Now, I have seen doubt do the opposite when it's experienced in isolation, away from humble, patient, and experienced youth workers who, like tour guides, point out things teens would have otherwise missed. But many young people don't feel safe to express these questions, so they hide them away and then, from our perspective, they suddenly and out of nowhere announce they've lost faith.

A few months ago, one of our teens got a part-time job. He was at our summer camp in DC and really had an amazing encounter with the Lord. But soon after camp this part-time job kept him from coming regularly to youth group. A couple of months of his inconsistent attendance went by, and so I set up a time to reconnect. And it was there over coffee that he told me he was looking deeper into Buddhism and that the Christian faith just wasn't making sense to him anymore. I dug a little deeper and found out that the things he was troubled by when it came to Christianity, I, also, was troubled by. You know, hypocrisy, judgmental Christians, the way many churches treat homosexuals, how politically affiliated the American church has become, how today's churches don't resemble the early church movement, and on and on.

He was shocked that I agreed with him, and then I asked, "What was it about the faith that initially drew you in?" As he started to share, I saw him begin to remember. And the more he shared, the more I saw him strengthened. By the end of the conversation, he had decided to change his work schedule so he wouldn't miss youth group as much as he was missing. Now, it's not a neat and tidy little bow at the end of the story—he's on a journey for sure—but it's amazing what open conversation can do. We know doubt in isolation can lead to a lost faith, but doubt within community actually benefits the community and leads the whole group into a deeper and more robust faith. Which is why we must begin to celebrate the questions and do our best to keep them alive.

I'm convinced that if questions aren't brought to our youth in love and with careful thoughtfulness, then their faith will be proven to be surprisingly fragile when they go away to college or, more likely, even sooner. We have to stop fearing the questions or rebuking their "out-there" ideas and show our teens a humble, engaged faith that is open, honest, and vulnerable and always ready to honor them wherever they're at.

I think we must even go a step further and make sure we are

keeping the questions alive. That we bring the questions to them without quickly resolving them, allowing our youth to actually struggle a bit within the community. Questions within the group will bring amazing depth. Now this is easy to say, but could possibly get you in hot water with parents. Parents' fears spike when their kids start asking questions and doubting and struggling with their faith. It's vital we carry the vision for a question-based dialogue, because this is what will help youth make their faith their own.

QUESTIONS AS PART OF THE JOURNEY

In the early 2000s we tended to just be the question-askers, allowing teens to land almost anywhere. It was the postmodern philosophy of youth ministry. I understood it and even embraced some of it, but to be honest, it never fully resonated with me. Much of it felt like wallowing in doubt or—at its worst—even antagonism.

It would go something like this:

> Youth: "I really believe in Jesus."
> Youth Pastor: "Why do you believe in him?"
> Youth: "Because it's what I've been taught by my parents."
> Youth Pastor: "Well, that's a lousy reason."
> Youth: "Oh?"
> Youth Pastor: "Yeah, I won."

Not really, but you get the idea. When I wrote my senior thesis in college about a thousand years ago, I wrote about how we can develop positive critical thinkers. At the time I was wondering if there was a happy medium, where we could help youth think critically about the world, about culture, and even about the faith. But I didn't think we needed to teach them to deconstruct everything they hear in a negative way. I hoped to develop positive people who also had eyes to see the good in surprising places.

Ultimately, we know what we must do, we must be about building up their most holy faith and that means we help them develop thought for their reasons. So yes, afflict the comfortable and comfort the afflicted, but do it all in love and with the intention of helping build a strong foundation of faith.

Thomas is one of my favorite characters in the Bible, and his questions, his doubts, were not rebuffed. They set him up to further his journey into radical faith.

_____

One of my wife's seminary professors is from the southern tip of India. He was born and raised in a region called Kerala. Kerala is one of the only regions in India that has a long history of Christianity. In fact, it goes back a couple thousand years because of a doubter-turned-missionary by the name of Thomas. But before Thomas hit the road telling everyone he came in contact with about his risen friend, something dramatic happened in his life that moved him from skepticism to being willing to die for that faith.

Let's quickly look at some of this together in John 20:

> *Now Thomas (also known as Didymus), one of the*
> *Twelve, was not with the disciples when Jesus came.*
> *So the other disciples told him,*
> *"We have seen the Lord."*
> *But he said to them, "Unless I see the nail marks in*
> *his hands and put my finger where the nails were, and*
> *put my hand into his side, I will not believe."*
> *A week later his disciples were in the house again,*
> *and Thomas was with them. Though the doors were*
> *locked, Jesus came and stood among them and said,*

"Peace be with you!" Then he said to Thomas, "Put
your finger here; see my hands. Reach out your hand
and put it into my side. Stop doubting and believe."
Thomas said to him, "My Lord and my God!"
Then Jesus told him, "Because you have seen me, you
have believed; blessed are those who have not seen
and yet have believed."
– John 20:24-29 (NIV)

First of all, Thomas had the nickname "Didymus," which means "the twin." Thomas—like many of us, whether we admit it or not—had a twin. A naughty twin; an opposite Thomas.

It kind of reminds me of George Costanza on *Seinfeld* and how he discovered that every natural inclination he ever had in his life was the wrong one. Every reaction, every decision he made was never right. So, he started doing everything the opposite of what he would naturally and normally do. Instead of seeing a girl and not walking up to her and talking to her (and then regretting it all day long), he would do the opposite. He would now walk up to her, talk to her, and admit he was balding, had no job, and was overweight—and of course this actually worked. The ladies loved this refreshingly honest George. Of course, he kept falling back into his old George ways, but when he could, opposite George emerged and saved the day—at least for one episode.

See, my twin loves chocolate milkshakes, red meat, and no exercise. While my other self is a vegetarian, despises refined sugar, and is a marathon runner. But my Didymus is always winning that battle. (Funny thing is that I'm in Starbucks right now writing this and sipping on a chocolate Frappuccino.)

Many of us have a church-self and then we have a private-self. Some of us have a triplet: we have a church-self, the home-self, and then the school- or work-self. Many teens may be quintuplets. They have multiple Georges.

But the point is clear, Thomas lived a dualistic life like all of us; and one life was willing to die with Jesus, according to John 11:16:

> *Then Thomas (also known as Didymus) said*
> *to the rest of the disciples,*
> *"Let us also go, that we may die with him."*
> *– **John 11:16 (NIV)***

But then he was also the guy who refused to believe in the risen Jesus even though his friends were pleading with him to believe. Still, this dualism must have been something that Jesus saw in him early on, and he knew that Thomas would eventually have to choose which self he would allow to emerge. And so, Jesus gave Thomas the extra push he needed by honoring Thomas's desire to see Jesus' scars for himself.

We can't forget what Jesus knew, that behind Thomas's doubt was a sincere desire to know truth personally. This is true of our youth who are growing up in the emerging post-Christian world. They really want God to be real, to be active and alive. They don't want to settle anymore for pat answers and other people's experiences; they must see this for themselves and experience it all for themselves. And we must honor them.

If you think about the Scripture passage a little more, this interaction could have gone very differently and changed Thomas's story forever. It could have ended up in a very different place. The disciples might have been offended by Thomas's doubt and his skepticism and rebuked him. Thomas could have left thinking, "I'm never coming back here again." Somehow the environment of the disciples wasn't a negative one, and then we see later that Jesus himself goes above and beyond and honors Thomas's questions, pursues him, and meets him in the midst of all of the doubt. This changed everything not only for him, but also for India.

After that day, Thomas was never called Didymus again. But Jesus took him through this beautiful discovery of uncovering who he really was, so that he could live fully into this new reality. He ended up traveling all the way down the coast of India telling people about the risen Jesus and how he was profoundly changed by him. He kept traveling, looking for open hearts and minds, and finally got to the people of Kerala, where my wife's professor was born and raised. There he found a receptive group—so much so that he ended up having to plant seven different churches just to keep up with the great multitudes of new believers. He eventually left that region and headed into a new area to plant an eighth congregation, when the leaders of that new region killed him for all the mess this new faith was causing.

I was speaking about Thomas at an event not long ago, and I mentioned the region called Kerala, where Thomas established those seven churches. After I spoke, a woman came up to me and said she was born and raised there and that her home church was one of the seven that Thomas planted. (Amazing.) She said the churches are all still thriving and the whole region is full of committed Jesus-followers. See, like our youth, Thomas wanted more than just warm feelings and an experience with Jesus; and he definitely wasn't looking for religion. There was a deep longing in Thomas to be a part of a movement, and it's what woke him up to living out his true identity.

In the story of Thomas, we see a kid becoming an adult. Right there in the Scriptures we see the adolescent journey taking place where Thomas unloads his childish and small-minded thinking and embraces a robust, category-shattering person by the name of Jesus. Massive excavation happens in the mind and life of Thomas. He moves from disbelief to belief, then into full on movement.

REBUILDING

With the emergence of post-Christianity, we see this now in profound ways. But many have heard this term and have wondered if it means the apocalypse is coming. I get that fear, but honestly, there is nothing to fear here. "Post-Christian" is actually a term C. S. Lewis used back in the 1950s in regard to Europe, and the United Kingdom in particular. He noticed that the dominant and most influential voices shaping culture were no longer Christian. And this is true of North America now.

I have the privilege of traveling around the country to speak to middle school, high school, and college students. Youth in the Northeast and youth in the South sound the same to me. They're asking very similar things, they're troubled by what they see in the church, and they're full of profound and beautiful questions. And perhaps this apocalypse, this demolition of the Christian church in the US, will mirror what is happening outside my window. It's an opportunity to rise up and rebuild on a better foundation for the sake of the generations to come. A foundation that will allow the history and traditions of the church to inform our confident humility as we wrestle alongside of our youth, honoring their doubts and questions the way Jesus honored Thomas's.

My wife, Kelsey, was in a room last weekend with a group of tenth-grade girls at our winter camp. All of them were talking about how they were sensing God and how they were being challenged in their thinking by the speaker (me). One girl, in the midst of all this talk of faith and renewed passion, really passionately interjected her frustration. The room was a bit stunned, especially because the speaker's wife was sitting there with them. After this young lady finished talking, my wife looked at her and said, "Oh wow, that is really good—I've been there, please tell us more about that."

She said it was amazing to see this girl explore her questions and slowly calm down, open up to the group, and allow other girls—who had obviously thought through the same questions—to impact her thinking. Afterwards one of our volunteers, who had a Young Life background, came up to my wife amazed. This leader couldn't believe how Kelsey stayed warm and invited more conversation rather than squashing it. Kelsey just kept digging for what was at the heart of the whole thing. She didn't leave the doubt alone but was curious and interested and remained unthreatened. By the end of that weekend, this girl's story took some dramatic steps toward Jesus.

Our job is to slowly and patiently escort teens toward mystery and faith and openness and to not be threatened by their passionate objections to people who say they've experienced the risen Jesus. We help youth, like Jesus helps Thomas, see that this faith is something worthy of building their lives on and that it will rise up within them as a beacon that will draw the world in.

Last year, I was one of the keynote speakers at a youth conference. The conference had me speak the third night about the cross. My goal was to reframe the gospel in a way that helped makes sense of the cross within the larger story. I ended by mentioning that the cross of Jesus was the very thing that led the first century into a revolution and that this revolution is the very thing God calls us into—a faith that is a movement of people doing the work of God in the world.

I was amazed by the response of the youth and could really feel them with me—you know, those nights where the room is warm with God's palpable presence and everyone is quietly on the edge of their seats. Now, I was only asked to give one

34

talk toward the end of the event, and so I was hoping the next speaker would kind of do a "now what" talk that next evening, continuing the idea of faith as a movement. Instead, however, he basically gave a sin management sermon. You know, how to go home and stop all that sinning. It was a talk all about what not to do when you got home. It was full of manipulation and guilt and condemnation and just noise. I was grieved. See, I felt like those teens were dying to know what their faith meant in their world, and they were longing to know how to get in on what God was already doing. They already knew what not to do, they were dying to know what *to* do. I wanted to walk up and interrupt the speaker at the end of his talk and say, "What this guy is saying is not what this whole thing is about. It's not the story you've been invited into. It's so much bigger than that." But I knew challenging the speaker in front of the youth was a jerk move.

So, instead, I just sat there quietly stewing in my frustration.

But afterwards I was hanging out in the lobby area where they wanted us to greet teens, and one of them came up to me and said, "Brock, I want to know more about the movement thing you mentioned. I'm just really longing for more."

I don't think he is alone in this feeling. Youth are longing for more than just an intellectual belief system. They're longing for more than a sin management program. They are longing for transcendence. They want to be a part of something greater than themselves, but we've turned this faith movement into a religious program, where youth feel like they aren't safe to make mistakes or ask questions or challenge stifling religious systems. What they've been given is not the faith. The faith is a movement, and it's made up of a group of people choosing to pick up their crosses daily for the sake of God's kingdom. The faith is something that empowers and calls us, like Thomas, to bring the most amazing news possible to a world desperate for a Savior.

*Jesus' resurrection is the beginning of God's new
project not to snatch
people away from earth to heaven but to colonize
earth with the life of heaven.
That, after all, is what the Lord's Prayer is about.*
**– N. T. Wright
*Surprised by Hope***

CHAPTER 2
SIT, WATCH, AND SLEEP

My parents dragged me to church constantly as a kid. But here's the weird thing, church never really resonated with me, even though I was there all the time. I just never fully understood what we were doing. I just didn't really get it. Maybe it isn't weird, because I've always sensed that I'm not alone in this. But it felt to me like a team in the locker room talking about the game plan or maybe a school at a pep rally. Only the team never actually gets out of the locker room and the school never actually gets on the buses to go to the game and participate.

Really, I think what it was is that my early childhood ruined me. I was born at the beginning of the Jesus movement in the early 1970s. My parents were in a Christian rock band, and so for about the first ten years of my life I lived on a tour bus going from town to town seeing teens joining the movement of Jesus. It was genuinely exciting, meaningful, and legitimately a revolution. Maybe you've heard about the Jesus movement in the past, but to get a full sense of the larger narrative, you have to go back into the 1950s, starting with the beatniks. And to understand the beatniks, you have to go back to the 1940s.

America entered World War 2 just after Pearl Harbor, in December of 1941. Thousands and thousands of young men enlisted for the war, and when they left home the women joined the workforce. This meant the children were kind of on their own, because there were no real systems in place to care for them. Imagine being a little kid and suddenly your dad is gone, and then your mom and all their moms—for the first time in American history—leave their homes to join the workforce. You and all the neighborhood kids are left to just make it on your own. This doesn't seem like a big deal because of the culture we live in today, but this was a massive shift in American life for families then. Still, everyone was sacrificing for the cause of freedom.

The war was gruesome, and many lives were lost. But evil was eventually slain; and in 1945, young young men returned home from the war and slept with their wives, who got pregnant. So, we had a huge baby boom in 1945. Why I tell you all of this is because something incredible started to happen just five years later in September of 1950, which is that classrooms were suddenly bursting with new students—millions more than ever before. In fact, I once heard a speaker at a national youth worker convention put the increase at six million—six million more children in kindergarten than previous years. So 1950 marked a major transition for schools all over the country. Leaders in education strategized a brand-new way of doing school. It was the divide and conquer method. American schools moved from one-room schoolhouses to grade-specific education. This is significant because this was the birth of the massive peer pressure phenomenon. See, before 1950, you'd have one teacher and a bunch of different-aged students in one room. The older students wouldn't just work on their own schoolwork but would help the younger students—it was a great environment for learning, with the older students being taught how to teach and mentor, as well as set the pace and atmosphere of the classroom. Now all of a sudden there was no depth, no student leaders, and only peer influence in each classroom.

So, you have to picture this for a moment. You have these older children who were running the streets while dad was away at war and while mom was working, and now you have these kindergartners whose dads are home from the war but are suffering from PTSD and are struggling to even cope. So, all these children were really hurting, lost, and just plain beat down. People noticed that they seemed aimless, apathetic, and rebellious. The country began to question the age-specific classrooms but wasn't sure of the way forward. Sociologists, reporters, and writers at the time began to call these kids the "beat-down" generation.

In and around 1958, thousands of teenagers were gathering in New York City, in Portland, in San Francisco, and all around the country; and a particular young man noticed this and saw that they were wide open for a movement. He was young Catholic poet and an American novelist by the name of Jack Kerouac, who had a heart for the youth of the late '40s and early '50s. He came in with a vision to reject the "beat-down" label the media and sociologists had stuck on this generation. He turned it on its head by calling them "beatniks," a group led by the spirit of the beatitudes.

Let me pause here for a second. This makes me think of our role as youth workers. How are youth being labeled today? How are they being described and identified?

> *Disengaged?*
> *Hurting?*
> *Addicted?*
> *Self-obsessed?*
> *Shallow?*

I wonder how we as youth workers can flip the switch on these labels and provide vision for a new and better way for our youth?

Now back to the beatniks and how Kerouac painted a beautiful vision for these young people. He clarified the cause of this teen movement, and at New York's Hunter College playhouse in 1958, Kerouac said, "It's because I am Beat, that is, I believe in beatitude and that God so loved the world that he gave his only begotten Son to it."[1] He went on to describe the beatitudes and how this generation would be known by them.

It's interesting to see Kerouac's impact on the whole beatnik scene. Even his passion for art and poetry had profound influence, as the beatnik generation embraced poetry and all forms of art by gathering in coffeehouses all over the country to read poetry to each other with a bongo player providing background, texture, and mood to the art form. In 1959, the TV show *Dobie Gillis* famously stereotyped the beatniks of the day and became the first series where the central characters were all teenagers. It was a light-hearted portrayal of sensitive teenagers who seemed like they were just kind of floating and hanging out together but were also passionate about what was happening in the world.

As the 1960s progressed, a disillusionment set in as many leaders of the movement began to die from drug overdoses or just disappeared and fell deep into ineffectiveness due to heroine and other hallucinogens or alcohol abuse. Even Kerouac fell away and died of the effects of alcoholism. This was all happening in the midst of the angsty teenage beatnik movement. But as these children got older, the beatniks became the hipsters, and the hipsters eventually morphed into the hippies of the mid-1960s. By this time, they had forgotten their core reason for existence and embraced a lesser version with free love, drug use, and a vague spirituality.

Movements like this are amazing—a multi-decade movement that began with youth in the mid- to late 1950s, forged by youth workers and visionaries like Kerouac leading the way. But it lost steam, like many movements, because they lost their first love. And just when the whole thing might have seemed like a loss, for nothing, something fortunate happened. A beautiful full circle took place in the late 1960s and on into the early 1970s that brought the teen movement back to the beatitudes with an even more robust embrace of Jesus.

In June of 1971, *Time Magazine's*[2] cover story, titled "The Jesus Revolution," was all about it. It was a phenomenon. Hundreds of thousands of teenagers all over the country were giving their lives to Jesus. What's cool about this story is that at the beginning of the Jesus movement in 1969, my parents started that hippie Jesus rock and roll band, which lasted through the 1970s. But like I said, it ruined me.

My parents' band played at the Billy Graham crusades to draw in teenagers, and we'd see thousands of young people come to the Lord. When not at the crusades we'd travel into a city and find the highest spot in town, and together we'd look over the whole of the city and pray that God would do an amazing work. Every week, just as *Time* said, multitudes were opening their lives to Christ. I remember as a little guy being filled with passion over the teens. But, it ruined me for status quo church living.

By the time the 1980s hit, the movement had ended for a variety of reasons, and my parents quit the band to become youth pastors. Going from the tour bus to the church was a difficult transition for me.

And I've often wondered what happened. Why did the movement end? So, we must ask similar questions about our current systems. What is causing the shrinking of the American church and youth groups? We all read stats about the disengagement of youth in the church and the utter disdain for the church by people outside of the church. It all just makes me wonder: *What is the new thing God wants to do in the midst of what is happening today?*

But thinking back about the Jesus movement, it really happened outside of the church. In fact, the church had nothing

43

to do with it, until the very end. I remember walking into the auditoriums with my parents' band and seeing church people burning their albums. There was fear on the part of the church because of the loud music, but mostly the fear stemmed from the fact that they couldn't control the movement.

See, teenagers are naturally gatherers, and it makes adults feel uncomfortable when there's a bunch of kids out and about expressing their passions. It's interesting how the church, when it got control of the movement, seemingly snuffed it out. Youth were gathering in cities, and initially adults were going to them to teach and inspire and direct. When the church got involved, we brought the teenagers away from their natural gathering places and had them sit in rows of chairs. We made them get haircuts and put shoes on and act "proper." The church has always had leanings toward a pharisaic mentality. Then we did the worst thing we ever could have done—we made the church a business.

THE STERILIZATION OF CHURCH

Last night my wife and daughter wanted us to watch the movie *You've Got Mail*. It's a classic starring Tom Hanks and Meg Ryan. Tom Hanks's character is a big business tycoon whose huge bookstore causes Meg Ryan's quaint little bookstore around the corner to go out of business. In a telling conversation, Tom Hanks's character looks at Meg Ryan and says, "It wasn't personal, it was just business."

Meg Ryan looks back at him and says, "What is that supposed to mean? I am so sick of that. All that means is that it wasn't personal to you. But it was personal to me. It's 'personal' to a lot of people. And what's so wrong with being personal, anyway? … Whatever else anything is, it ought to begin by being personal."
Personal should be king.

But the church went and hired businessmen and businesswomen, with no heart for the very real personal/relational aspects of ministry, to put metrics in place to measure whether or not we were having success. They polished us all up and turned the church into a well-oiled machine. And we bought it hook, line, and sinker. Our churches became one-stop shopping with something for the whole family—complete with bookstores and coffeehouses—but we lost something in the process. The church became a sterile environment where a hippie or a street kid or an ordinary person would never feel comfortable. But this is what happens when comfort becomes your god. It makes everyone else really uncomfortable.

Now, I don't want to pooh-pooh the whole thing. I've been a big part of some of this. There have been some really good things that have taken place. The 1990s brought amazing things in the way of youth ministry. But on the whole, the sterilization of the church has had its effects.

I was thinking back recently about why I struggled so much when my parents quit the band. I struggled socially, academically, and even spiritually, with my faith. But I remember in the mid-1980s when I was in eighth grade, I heard the gospel at youth group in a way that just so resonated. The way the speaker spoke about the faith, it completely reminded me of my childhood. What he described was a movement. He explained that God was on the move and was calling us to join him. So, I went forward and reaffirmed my faith in Jesus, but I soon realized I wasn't really signing up for a movement. I was signing up to sit back down in rows and just talk about faith for the rest of my life. And I noticed that salvation to most of the Christians I knew meant the next life and it had nothing to do with *this* life. On top of all that, I gathered that I was signing up to no longer have fun—like the faith was all about not. doing. stuff.

When I went forward…

> I thought I was signing up for mission—that interested
> me.
> I thought I was signing up for a life empowered by God
> himself.
> I thought I was signing up for true community.
> I thought I was signing up for a life that love, joy,
> peace, faithfulness, gentleness, kindness,
> goodness, forbearance, and self-control
> just bubbled out of.
> I thought I was joining a cause that would bring those
> things to others and invite them into a life of
> meaning and significance.

That is what interested me.

But I felt like what I received was a bait and switch. They told
me following Jesus was an adventure, but then after I asked
Christ into my life they told me to be quiet and just listen and
be a good little boy.

Don't get me wrong, I loved hearing about Jesus living an
amazing life—living a life the way it was meant to be lived and
then inviting everyone to join him. And then Jesus and those
he invited actually went places and did things—even scary, not
comfortable things, but I loved hearing about that.

I was drawn to that. If you read the stories of Jesus, literally
thousands joined him. They followed him. They fully believed
and they followed him with great risk.

It was a struggle, this following Jesus thing.

Man, it's a struggle now, you know, actually following Jesus.
Not just with your mind, but with your feet and with your

voice. You wouldn't know that it's hard to actually follow Jesus by listening to many preachers today. You get the idea that the faith is pretty easy, it doesn't require much. And I'm not talking about legalism, I'm talking about living the way of Jesus and representing the reign of Christ, extending it everywhere you go.

Youth are made for such movements.

About fifteen years ago I started researching youth movements around the globe. That's when I ran into Alpha and the 24-7 Prayer movement in England. Literally, these movements are mostly outside of the church and are seeing large numbers of young people opening their lives to the way of Jesus in the here and now.

I recently took my team to the church in London that birthed the organization Alpha, to just see what they were doing. My team came in thinking the faith was dead in Europe only to discover just the opposite. I was talking with a European youth worker and asked her what was happening and why the faith is currently exploding in young people there.

She said three things. She said:

> It's mostly outside of the walls of the church and in their world.
> It's empowered and led by the youth themselves.
> It's wide open to the Holy Spirit.

Wow. Kind of sounds like a movement I want to be a part of.

Infuse your life with action.
Don't wait for it to happen.
Make it happen. Make your own future.
Make your own hope. Make your own love.
And whatever your beliefs, honor your Creator, not by
passively waiting for grace to come down from upon
high, but by doing
what you can to make grace happen...
yourself, right now, right down here on earth.
– Bradley Whitford
University of Wisconsin Commencement
Address 2004

CHAPTER 3
THE 2027 TEEN

It was in the 1950s that C. S. Lewis stood in front of a British audience and announced that truly all of Europe had slipped into a post-Christian era.[3] That is, the primary voices that were shaping language and culture were no longer Judeo-Christian. It's been interesting for me to follow and study the journey Europe has taken since and, in particular, to watch how the church dealt with their loss of influence and their reaction to being dismissed as culturally irrelevant.

I spent some time talking with my friend Simon, who became a Christian in the '90s during what was the beginning of a reawakening in England, an awakening back to the heart of Jesus. Simon was a young musician in London, and he grew up like many other Brits, an outright atheist. We met at our favorite Korean restaurant here in the DC area as he began to tell me his journey that shed so much light on what the United States is currently living through. He's a good friend and now the worship leader at our church. He somehow stumbled into a church in the heart of England as a young atheist and discovered some really good, life-altering news. But before this, England had been on a downward spiritual slope for many years.

See, after C. S. Lewis made his pronouncement, the church in the UK began what we see happening now in the United States. The church saw what was happening, saw the culture—especially during what was known as the sexual revolution of the 1960s. They were not only disturbed by what they were seeing, especially with the young, but they also saw themselves losing influence culture-wide—in education, government policymaking, and in political influence. They were losing their voice.

Now when the primary voice that has helped shaped culture and a people's way of thinking and life for hundreds of years begins to lose its power, it can get pretty ugly and downright scary. In fact, a culture war typically gets declared, and that is what has been happening in the United States for some time now. What the UK church went through in the 1950s on into the 1970s is what the North American church has been going through for at least ten to fifteen years now.

But the process begins with the church losing its voice. Like a bully who is no longer getting his way because he's lost the respect and fear of those around him, the church began to throw a temper tantrum. This is what happened in England, and if you turn on the news today in the US you will see much of the same. Loud and angry Republicans, many of whom consider themselves Christian, are desperately trying their darnedest to hold on to the past—a past that had them at the forefront of political policymaking with James Dobson and Jerry Falwell leading the way. Yes, angry and loud liberals—fearing the extreme right's agenda—are yelling and bashing their opposition too. But we are really seeing it from the Christian right currently because of how they had linked arms with the Republican party several decades ago.

But the British church—after some time of kicking and screaming in similar circumstances—realized they no longer had clout among the citizens of England, so they then began to turn inward. That is what you do when people "out there" stop listening to you. You turn to the insiders and moan, groan, and complain about how everyone is wrong and you're right.

See, the first response by the church with the emergence of post-Christianity here has been like that bully, who just gets louder and then tries hard to scare people into listening to them again. But of course we all know what happens—the bully gets dismissed. The people see the bully as weak and pathetic; a backward, angry, ignorant, and prejudiced person they no longer need to waste time with.

And now this is what is happening on a full scale in the States today. Like I said, the church has turned in on themselves and has begun to preach to the choir, declaring the world is going to hell in a handbasket—whatever that is. They are forgetting who they are as God's elect, called to bring hope and peace and good news to the world, not judgement and condemnation. They have been chosen to serve the world by being salt and light, to love and not hate, to have hope and not hold on to and push fear. But the truth is they forgot that long ago.

Power will do that to you, and so the losing of power just might be the best thing possible for God's people. This actually proved to be the case in Europe. (But we'll get to that soon enough.)

By the mid-1970s and on into the 1980s, the church in England became at best forgotten, at worst they became absolutely irrelevant. The idea of visiting a church became a common joke and a punchline on late-night TV. That is where the church was at the beginning of the 1990s in England. But then something beautiful happened.

A church in London realized that culture was having its impact on their people and that they were hurting, confused, and biblically illiterate. So, that's when they came up with Alpha, just to go over the basics of Christianity with their congregants. Everyone in the church went through the course, including the youth, and something odd and unexpected happened. These church people started getting saved. Imagine that, church people opening their lives up to Jesus in a new and fresh way. And after a couple of times of running the course they noticed something else was happening. Their church people started bringing their friends and those friends were opening their lives up to Jesus. This was a phenomenon for a community that had been steeped in the post-Christian culture for almost fifty years. They then decided what they had was actually for the whole city.

See, what they had was really good and freeing news for the world. This world there in England and the rest of Europe was broken and desperate for something with hope and substance. They were desperate for something deeply intelligent and beautifully spiritual. And the church was remembering what their role was for the world. No longer angry but full of compassion, they reached out with a transformative message.

My friend Simon was brought to that church by a friend when he was in a desperate place. He not only found Jesus, he found his calling and eventually became the worship pastor at this same church. But I have been thinking about what happened to Europe for all those years when they didn't have a decent access point to God. The church was not being what it was meant to be. Once the church reemerged as a place of blessing to the world, that very broken world was then ready to receive what it was longing for.

I look at the United States today and I see a world that is moving further and further into post-Christianity. I see a world that is desperate for some really good news, but the world—for the most part—may not be able to receive it from a church that is perceived to be angry and small-minded and judgmental.

But look at where the world is today. The world is a much different place for a kid to grow up in than it was for me as a teenager.

POST-CHRISTIAN WORLD REALITIES

There's a teen in my youth group I've been meeting with every week. He is full of anxiety, fears, and has broken relationships at home with all his siblings and parents. He can hold it together at school, for the most part, but when he walks into his home, he just crumbles and falls apart. Recently we were sitting in my office when he told me he'd just been diagnosed with OCD that week. He said he thinks he's a germaphobe as well. I sat there overwhelmed by him and all the other teens in our group who have unprecedented fear and anxiety.

Many are calling this the fear generation. I've been overwhelmed as a youth pastor by it all. With the emergence of technology and screens, everywhere you turn in our world people are losing the ability to just sit, to be still, to wait, and to just be. Watch a teen in your group text a friend. If the teen doesn't get a return text within thirty seconds, he or she will typically start freaking out. Technology is truly changing us and our habits in massive ways. Not only is our world losing the ability to find peace with moments of solitude and stillness, but the idea of quiet and stillness is becoming almost unthinkable.

Just this morning I heard some tragic news. Chris Cornell, the lead singer of Soundgarden passed away. This was one of my favorite bands in the 1990s, and the crazy thing is that for some of us that doesn't seem so long ago. But, wow, has the world changed so much since those days.

Let's think about how the pornography delivery system has changed. I began college in the 1990s before the Internet was even a thing. Pornography was somewhat accessible but, in fact, I never even looked at it. I was too much of a "good boy" to ever walk into a store to purchase it, not that I didn't want to. But today we have sixth graders coming into our middle school groups already addicted and with that comes massive sexual confusion. And it's not just our boys. This is causing the rewiring of our brains and minds and leading teens down very dark paths much earlier than ever before.

This is what a world of people look like who do not have the Holy Spirit empowering them every day with his fruit: love, joy, peace, faithfulness, kindness, goodness, gentleness, forbearance, and self-control. Our world could really use some of that fruit.

But that's not all, with a post-Christian world in full swing we see there is an inability to be good neighbors who are peacemakers in the world. You see it in the burst of extreme nationalism that is revealing itself in the news media and even on ordinary street corners. This past Saturday was Kelsey's and my twenty-second wedding anniversary. We went to Williamsburg, Virginia, and stayed at a resort overnight to celebrate. As soon as we got there, we threw on our bathing suits and headed out to the pool. I was laying on one of those poolside loungers sipping on a piña-colada when a gentleman walked by me with a t-shirt that said, "Veterans Before Refugees." My immediate thought was: "Can't we do both?" Can't we take care of our veterans and also love and care for the suffering and displaced of the world?

Extreme nationalism forgets all the Scripture passages that tell us as God's people how we are to treat refugees, that Jesus himself was a stranger in a strange land, and we must remember that the world is watching us as the church.

Youth are dying for a faith that doesn't just impact them as an individual but has a heart for their friends, their schools, their cities, their world. And they don't just want a faith that talks, they want a faith that walks—they want to belong to a movement that is making a difference in the world and breaking down walls that separate and divide. They want to be a part of radical and holy hospitality that is good news for every tongue, tribe, and nation.

So, like the people of Europe in the early 1990s, they are broken and ripe for some good news. The problem is they don't think there is a place for them in the church. They are messy and they feel the impact culture and their habits are having on their lives. When they look at the church in the United States, they see a bully who has been dethroned but is still kicking and screaming and throwing a tantrum rather than allowing the loss of respect to bring about much needed change. And so we have a marketing problem, a problem with perception that I fear is all too true. Heck, we don't even treat our own well. Recently I received an email from a parishioner in our church. The email was nice enough, honestly, but it had a warning with it. This gentleman said people had noticed I'd liked a Facebook post that promoted a conference where one of the many speakers was Rob Bell. The email went on to say people in our church had noticed and were "talking."

"Talking?" I thought, "Who cares." But as I read the email I realized that I'm not even safe in my own church. (I can't even imagine what Rob Bell is going through.) It's funny that the bully church can't get over themselves and just agree to disagree on some things. To show grace and listen and not feel threatened by differing opinions.

But there the world is, ready for a friend to show up without condemnation, just ready to listen and then humbly speak some pretty stinkin' good news to them. Remember, that's what we have after all. We aren't moralists or Pharisees, we're followers of Jesus. And as 1 Peter 5 tells us, our God is "the God of all grace."

I looked in the Greek and discovered something amazing about that passage—*all* literally means "all." What a name, what a title. Our God is the God of All Grace, but for whatever reason we can't seem to even show grace to each other. No wonder the world is having a hard time with us. This is what it was like in the 1970s and 1980s in the church in England. But then they remembered their calling to be bearers not of bad news but of good news.

As I was talking with Simon about the first time he walked into that church, he said he immediately just knew he was in the right place. Immediately he felt the presence of God, and that palpable presence was all he needed to know that they had something he was desperate for. He didn't hear condemnation, he already knew he was broken. They didn't need to waste his (or their) time speaking about how wrong he was. They instead had an air of confidence in the way of Jesus—confidence that the way of Jesus actually brings the peace he and others were so desperate for.

We don't need to worry another second about losing the culture war and making sure the world knows they're wrong. Instead what Simon and thousands and thousands of others were hearing was how the gospel changes everything and how they were tenderly loved and how a life with Jesus just flat out leads to a better way.

See, the truth is my friend I told you about in the introduction was right. We are catching up with the UK and are now only about ten years behind them. But they made some amazing strides in those ten years. They remembered what their role was as God's people. I believe if we make strides toward living out the way of Jesus in the world, ten years from now we'll see a difference. But we have to seize this opportunity to completely change our reputation and, as youth workers, train our youth in what it really looks like to be salt and light in a world desperate for flavor, clarity, and illumination.

Yes, we're going further and further into post-Christianity, and yes, many have been lost over the years. The church is seeing a mass exodus, especially by our young. I even have a dear friend who was a youth pastor for many years who is now the humanist chaplain at a major university. But our response to all of this is what will make all the difference in the world.

One of my favorite things about our church's services is that we always pray a prayer of confession. Every one of us says the same words, and it completely levels the playing field from the get-go. If you've walked into our church feeling like you don't belong, well, this prayer helps you and all of us know that we are all in need; we all need God's goodness in desperate ways.

Prayer of Confession

*Most merciful God, we confess that we have
sinned against you in thought, word, and deed,
by what we have done and what we have left undone.
We have not loved you with our whole heart;
we have not loved our neighbors as ourselves.
We are truly sorry and we humbly repent.
For the sake of your Son Jesus Christ,
have mercy on us and forgive us;
that we may delight in your will, and walk in your
ways, to the glory of your name. Amen.*
– The Book of Common Prayer

See, as the world's people become more and more addicted and broken, our response as the bearers of good news is to take the role of healers, hope-givers, and become a sanctuary, a people of peace—knowing we ourselves are addicted and broken and in desperate need of God's constant working in our lives. Oh, this role is a difficult one for sure, but what an honor to point people with our lives and with our words to the great restorer of life.

Character cannot be developed in ease and quiet.
Only through experience of trial and suffering can the
soul be strengthened, ambition inspired,
and success achieved.
– Helen Keller

CHAPTER 4
SUFFERING AS A WAY FORWARD

He stood in front of the whole church that Sunday morning and told his story about how at our houseboats camp he had discovered Jesus in a life-changing and profound kind of way. There wasn't a dry eye in the place. I sat in the front row with tears in my eyes, listening as he described how God had delivered him from addiction and how he would never be the same again. Down deep, I knew the struggle in his life was far from over, but I, as a young youth worker, was just hoping for the best.

Our youth ministry then took a few weeks off for most of the month of August to take a breather and to gear up and plan for the busy fall months, and when our fall kick-off happened, this teen was conspicuously missing. He was someone who never missed, and he was missed. I called him later that week but didn't get through, so I left a message. This went on for a number of weeks. Finally, he reluctantly agreed to meet me for coffee. We sat there for a few minutes making small talk, but I was bursting inside. So, I finally asked, "Dude, what's going on?"

Looking down, he said, "Brock, I just don't believe anymore."

"Tell me more about that," I said.

"I don't know," he answered. "I got back from the houseboats camp only to fall back into my addictions, and it led me to look around the world and see all the horrible things out there. I just don't think that if I were God I'd let all of this continue. I just can't believe anymore."
I understood, I had been there myself. And I felt like I had set

him up for failure. See, this was a young person primed for a movement, but I didn't ready him for the days and weeks and months ahead. I gave him an easy gospel. And even though I was young, I should have known better.

There was a period in my life where I was really questioning the faith. Most of us go through times where we question what we've been taught, what we believe, and wonder if it still holds water for the ever-changing world. When I went through a very dark period in my life it led me to some of those same questions:

> *God, where the heck are you?*
> *Why would you let this happen?*
> *Is any of this really even true?*
> *Can I really trust the Scriptures or you?*

These kinds of questions came flooding into my heart and mind at that time. It's amazing how hard stuff can shake us and can cause us to question everything we know about God.

Looking back at the gospel messages I heard growing up, it was for the most part a gospel that taught me that once I became a Christian, God would protect me, be there for me, bless me, and lead me into happiness. Now people didn't use those exact words, but I don't think I'm the exception. I think what I heard is kind of the rule, especially here in America. Somehow the American dream and the faith got in bed together, and it screwed everything up.

I was sitting in a seminar recently and the speaker said what we all know to be true but don't really know what to do with. She said, "The number one reason kids leave the faith is because of suffering." Hard things come and today's churches preach a gospel that barely resembles that of the early church followers of Jesus. It just doesn't sound much like the writers' Gospels. I just think we have to ready our youth and even call them into a life where suffering lives. Because it seems like suffering just might be the very thing that produces a choice, fragrant fruit in us.

I love Romans 5:3-5.

> *Not only so, but we also glory in our sufferings, because we know that suffering produces perseverance; perseverance, character; and character, hope. And hope does not put us to shame, because God's love has been poured out into our hearts through the Holy Spirit, who has been given to us.*
> **– Romans 5:3-5 (NIV)**

When you look at the very difficult world teenagers are trying to navigate through, you see that suffering is just a part of teenage life. Heck, it's just part of life in general, no matter what age you are. But if you're not ready for it, a loss of faith is waiting for you. If you don't hang in there, through all the hard stuff of life *with* God, you may never get to that hope that's promised to never disappoint. It's just too easy to bail before the good stuff emerges. But I get it, it's hard to see the forest for the trees when you're in deep.

THE PROBLEM WITH CERTAINTY

I began a habit about fifteen years ago of reading at least one book a year from an atheist, agnostic, or from someone thoughtful outside of the faith. I find that it keeps me thinking, on my toes, relevant, and it humbles me. I remember when I picked up Bart Ehrman's book, *God's Problem*. I was so struck by his story. Ehrman is kind of the poster child for agnosticism, and he's the religious studies professor at the University of North Carolina Chapel Hill. His story, for us youth workers, is very interesting to track with. In his book, *Misquoting Jesus*, he talks about how as a teenager he was certain the Christian faith was completely true and every word of the Bible was divinely inspired. Again, he was certain of this.

I love what Anne Lamott says about certainty. She says, "The opposite of faith is not doubt, but certainty."[4] It's funny because I have found my most certain youth group teens are the ones who end up struggling the most with faith during the college years.

But Ehrman became a Christian as a teenager and then went to the great Wheaton College. He felt like God was calling him into ministry, and so he finished at Wheaton and then went on to Princeton to get his MDiv and PhD. But he talks about how the more he studied, the more he began to question the faith altogether. By the time he approached his '40s he had left the faith completely and embraced agnosticism and a soft atheism. I say "soft" because his wife is still a believer and this no doubt has an impact on his respect for faith.

And what sent Ehrman away from God was that he wasn't sure what to do with all of the suffering in the world. Again, this is the number one reason young people leave the faith. It's a major player in what is keeping them from the movement. They look at the world and see all the brokenness, the pain, and tragedy; and they can't figure out how a loving God would allow—or worse, cause—all the suffering in the world. I use the word *cause* because this is what they hear over and over again at church. When someone is suffering, they hear the disgusting pat answers of Christian people saying, "It's all part of God's plan," or some other confusing mumbo-jumbo. And they think, "Really? God's plan is that that little girl got abducted and forced into prostitution? This is what God's plan is?"

Even the softer version that "God allows these things" can be a rough one to work through, unless there is an adult there to journey through the mental gymnastics of it all. When we offer pat answers and then a theology of certainty, this can lead youth into discouragement, confusion, and a full abandonment of their faith.

Ehrman's journey was…

Doubt → Faith → Certainty → Doubt → Loss of Faith

What's amazing to look at is how the writers of the New Testament and the early church followers of Jesus understood suffering. They knew they lived in a broken world and that people suffered because of it. They also knew there was an enemy who played a major role in the world. And in the midst of it all, they still chose to follow Jesus knowing full well it would naturally lead them into extreme hardship. They were so convinced of God's love, they knew that despite the evil intentions of the enemy or of other human beings—and despite the natural brokenness of the universe—God would work things out in the end. He would mysteriously take all the horror in the world and make it right one day. Did they fully understand it? No. They were okay with living in the tension of it all, and they fully embraced mystery without feeling the need to have all their questions answered.

If you look back at Peter's story in the Scriptures, he denied knowing Jesus to avoid suffering. But later he knew that an embrace of suffering was what could actually lead him and others into a deeper place of faith. In fact, when you look at Peter's reinstatement, just after Jesus' resurrection on the beach, Jesus tells him that if he joins the movement, one day they will "stretch his hands" like they did Jesus' on the cross and kill him. Then Jesus says, "Follow me."

That's not an easy gospel.

But eventually Peter gets it and he begins to look at suffering differently. He begins to call people to join the movement in spite of it. Rather than explain suffering away, dismiss it, or offer ridiculous pat answers, he embraced mystery and called people into a way of living that might bring hard times, even death. (What a completely different perspective than us Westerners have.) Now, there are a couple of reasons we suffer, Peter says: 1) because we do stupid things; and 2) because we follow Jesus and it brings hardship.

Look at 1 Peter 4:12-19 with me:

> *Dear friends, do not be surprised at the fiery ordeal that has come on you to test you, as though something strange were happening to you. But rejoice inasmuch as you participate in the sufferings of Christ, so that you may be overjoyed when his glory is revealed. If you are insulted because of the name of Christ, you are blessed, for the Spirit of glory and of God rests on you. If you suffer, it should not be as a murderer or thief or any other kind of criminal, or even as a meddler. However, if you suffer as a Christian, do not be ashamed, but praise God that you bear that name. For it is time for judgment to begin with God's household; and if it begins with us, what will the outcome be for those who do not obey the gospel of God? And,*
> *"If it is hard for the righteous to be saved, what will become of the ungodly and the sinner?" So then, those who suffer according to God's will should commit themselves to their faithful Creator and continue to do good.*
> **– 1 Peter 4:12-19 (NIV)**

This passage is so practical for our youth. Peter was reconciling the experience of suffering for new followers of Christ, who had this new faith. They were inclined to believe when they experienced pain in life that maybe God was punishing them or maybe they weren't God's people after all. Sound familiar? They thought that if we were really God's children and he was loving and good, they wouldn't be suffering so much.

Last night I received a phone call at around eleven o'clock. It was one of our high school guys and he was really struggling. He apologized for calling me so late, but then went on to explain how his dad had been making fun of him for believing in Jesus. His dad is a strong atheist and is really disappointed that his son would believe such "nonsense." So, his dad had walked into his bedroom about an hour earlier and berated him. For an hour, he had belittled his faith to the point where they were both screaming at each other. This amazing young man said to me over the phone, "It just doesn't seem worth it, and maybe my dad is right."

Honestly, that's hardship. Sure, it's no burning at the stake, crucifixion, or even what Christians are going through in the Middle East right now; but this guy was really hurting and confused. Just like Peter's audience, he was surprised there was struggle after entering into a relationship with Jesus. Today's young person wonders what in the world is going on and then will extend it to the entire world by asking, "Why does God let bad things happen to good people?"

The early Christians lived in a culture that was, similar to our own, becoming adverse to their faith and no longer sympathetic. Peter, in these verses, addresses suffering because it was just so pivotal for these new and, most likely, young followers of Jesus. Peter offers those who trusted God a countercultural viewpoint of suffering that the current culture, philosophies, and religions could not supply: *Suffering is evidence of your faith and suffering does not have the final word.*

There are a few topics the Protestant church does not address very well with their young people and with the greater church as a whole. One of those is singleness and the other is what we're talking about right now—suffering. The American dream has so supplanted the kingdom of God in our thinking that we have sold our youth a false paradigm within which to practice their faith. Suffering always has been and always will be a cornerstone to deeper intimacy with Christ as we identify with him in his sufferings.

Just as we must have a theology of new life and healing, we must also embrace suffering and somehow hold them both together for our youth so that when times get tough they don't fall, they don't give in to poor characterizations of who God is, and will instead allow God to use the difficult to demonstrate his goodness. Peter understood that and did a brilliant job at relocating suffering within a better story.

SUFFERING AND A SOVEREIGN CREATOR

I remember when my daughter went through a period of extreme anxiety. It got so bad that she would hear what sounded like a loud train at full steam running in her mind. I remember holding her as she cried and suffered. It was a daily grind for quite a few years. But two days ago at our middle school camp she spoke to our youth about the mind and giving Christ your thoughts and allowing him to reign. She spoke about her struggle and how those years my wife and I journeyed with her brought us closer together and how together we pursued Jesus, even when it was hard. I couldn't believe the wisdom and clarity she spoke with. I knew we were giving our youth a proper view of this life and how God's name is *Emmanuel*—he is the God who goes with us through the storm. She even said she was grateful for the struggle. That she found God in a much more intimate way than if she never would have suffered at all.

When you look at the early church you discover that what drew many into the fold of the movement was the way the Christians were handling suffering in their time. Their culture was not compassionate toward this new sect of Jewish Christ-followers—and certainly not receptive to all these Gentiles being welcomed into the fold. They were strange, different, and easily blamed for whatever ailed the citizenry. They suffered at the hands of the rulers—real suffering, both physical and emotional. At times their very lives were at stake, so they really knew and understood what suffering was.

Sometimes we in the West are so far removed from this kind of suffering at the hands of the powerful that we grow complacent and self-reliant. These early Christians did not have that luxury. But there was also a personal suffering, as the apostle Paul indicates by mentioning his thorn in the flesh. This is where many of us can relate to some extent, and it's also the category my daughter and many of our youth fall into. It's hard to find a young person today who has not had at least one major, debilitating thorn in the flesh at some point. Our circumstances may look different than the early believers', but as broken and suffering individuals trying to reconcile our loving God with the incredibly painful circumstances of our lives, we share a common concern.

The way suffering is viewed by the culture plays an important role. Peter was able to offer up a better way, full of meaning and transformative power. You see, Peter wrapped the Creator God around suffering. This is the polar opposite of the philosophies of that day, which embraced blind fate as the dictator of our lives. If fate is in control of our destinies, then we're at its whim. Life is not ordered and has no meaning. If fate is blind, there is chaos created by an impersonal entity, wholly uninterested in us personally.

But if there is a Creator, a God who put things together with intention, then there is order over chaos, and meaning in life. A faithful creator (1 Peter 4:19) is one in whom you can place your trust. If I "suffer according to God's will" (v. 19, NIV), there is no room for "blind fate" to influence our lives as though we're a paper boat being tossed around on the ocean. Instead there is meaning to suffering, and we are headed in a direction that will be for good.

Today's naturalistic view, which has permeated our culture, rings strikingly similar to the philosophies combated by Peter's letters. Take this quote out of atheist Richard Dawkins's book, *River Out of Eden: A Darwinian View of Life*:

> "The total amount of suffering per year in the natural world is beyond all decent contemplation… In a universe of electrons and selfish genes, blind physical forces and genetic replication, some people are going to get hurt, other people are going to get lucky, and you won't find any rhyme or reason in it, nor any justice. The universe that we observe has precisely the properties we should expect if there is, at bottom, no design, no purpose, no evil, no good, nothing but pitiless indifference."[5]

Essentially, Dawkins is revealing to us a similar fatalistic philosophy that espouses no meaning to suffering beyond the meaning we choose to assign to it. Once again we're saddled with the feeling that we're being tossed around only to be supplanted by the "fittest." There is no redemptive quality to suffering, according to Dawkins, no hope for some sort of greater good to come out of it. So, as you can see, our youth are living under similar philosophical questions as the early church, and they are asking, "How does a good and loving God allow suffering?"

So, if we understand that suffering is the result of evil and sin, not God, we begin to get a glimpse of the complexity of it all. Especially knowing God can use evil against evil and transform it into something good on behalf of humanity and all of creation. That's what it means to be sovereign—that despite evil's best, he can take it and eventually bring beauty out of it.

One of the greatest evidences of this is the evil and injustice of Jesus' death. Most of us would say his death was the most lavish display of God's great love for us, the best thing that could have happened to us in time and eternity. There's mystery to be embraced here. Or even look at Paul's thorn in the flesh: "In my weakness God's grace is sufficient" (2 Corinthians 12:9, author's paraphrase). There's meaning to all of this in God's economy. He uses our suffering for good and for a purpose.

GOD WITH US

So, it was about 11:15 that night, and I was exhausted listening to this young man over the phone describe the pain he felt because of his father. I listened prayerfully. I whispered under my breath, "God, give me your words."

Then he said, "Brock, can you help me?"

"I'm just so proud of you." I said. "This is really hard and I'm so glad you called. The amazing thing is that the Scriptures even tell us to expect suffering when we say yes to Jesus. We're supposed to expect suffering from a world that sees the faith as foolishness. Your dad sees this whole thing as foolishness. But God... he is going to use this. He was with you in that bedroom and he doesn't want this to destroy you. He even put it in your heart to call me. He doesn't want you going through this alone. And he's going to take all of this— all of your pain and all of my pain—and he's going to use it to bring something amazing out of it. Something deep and beautiful that can be used to help others. God didn't cause

73

this, but he will take our pain and use it to wake us up. When we struggle, we become awakened to the craziness of our self-sufficiency. We wake up to our utter need for the God who was actually with you in your bedroom as your dad was attacking you. Jesus is with you in this, and you are actually participating with Jesus, and the Spirit rests upon you. Jesus went into the depths of suffering on the cross, and when you suffer for Jesus—which is what you just experienced—there is never anything more intimate with God than that. I'm just so proud of you. And I'm with you."

I know you can't live on hope alone; but without hope,
life is not worth living. So you, and you and you: you
got to give them hope; you got to give them hope.
– Harvey Milk

CHAPTER 5
YOUTH WORK AS ADVOCACY

L ast night we had our summer kickoff party as a
youth group. It was a blast with games, food, tie-dye
shirt-making stations, and the water sprinkler system from the
church to run and cartwheel through. You should have seen our
middle schoolers completely drenched, some in long denim
pants. (Can you say chafing?) But it was awesome, chafing and
all. After the fun, I spoke on courage and how God is calling
each of us to write an amazing story of courage with our lives.
Courage comes in many forms and can look many different
ways. I was talking about how courage might mean asking for
help, or admitting guilt, or welcoming a stranger, or standing
up for someone, or following Jesus in thoughtful ways at our
schools and workplaces. But I also mentioned that, however it
gets played out in our everyday, it will require us to embrace
discomfort.

When I finished my talk and began cleaning up from the event
with our team, a mother came up to me and asked if I'd come
over to her car to give her daughter a hug. I shrugged and said,
"Of course."

Now, here's a little background about this girl: There's history
here. My wife and I have been meeting with her and her
parents regularly all year long. This girl is overwhelmed with
debilitating anxiety. I walked up to the passenger-side window
and saw that her face was buried in her lap and she was crying.
I softly knocked on the door and asked if I could give her
a hug. She immediately jumped out and fell into my arms
weeping. Then with broken words she said, "I just can't do this
anymore. I can't handle all the pressure. Brock, I need help,
won't someone help me?"

Now here's what I've discovered within the last ten to fifteen years of youth ministry: We have an anxiety epidemic. (No duh.) And it's a plague that hasn't just swept the cities of the Northeast and the Southwest, but is in every small town, suburb, and urban place alike. I speak all over the country, and I've been listening to teens. It really doesn't matter the location; I keep hearing the same thing: "Brock, I feel like I just can't go on anymore."

In fact, I'm speaking at a camp right now in South Carolina, and I sat at a table full of students last night for dinner. All we were talking about was how riddled they are with anxieties and fears and debilitating hurt. See, the first thing we must do is listen, because when we do, we'll hear the heart behind what is below the surface of whatever outward persona a teen is portraying.

As a side note: Two years ago we took our youth to summer camp. One afternoon I was having one of those amazing conversations that seem to always happen at camp, with about fifteen high schoolers from our group, my daughter being one of them. This was before my daughter's issues with anxiety, and I remember asking how many of them were stressed out and overwhelmed with anxiety because of school. Every single teen raised his or her hand—all of them—except for one, my daughter. Now as a youth pastor I was happy to see that my girl wasn't struggling with even a smidgen of worry about school; but as a father, my first thought was, "Well, you could maybe use a little bit of stress, I mean just a little bit…"

She's just so wonderfully laid back, maybe too laid back, if you know what I mean. The reality is that the following year was the one that was very difficult for her for various reasons, and we did have to deal with the anxiety I described earlier and even depression to a small degree. Even she has not been unscathed. Youth today are overwhelmed.

But it's not just anxiety, there's struggle of all forms. We took our middle school youth away for a weekend retreat this past year, and on Saturday evening—the night we all book Jesus to show up—I spoke about what it really means to follow him. As I was speaking I saw a couple of them sleeping, some not paying attention, and I just didn't feel like anything was happening. (Hmm… maybe my admin forgot to make sure Jesus did, in fact, get booked for that evening's program?) I finished my talk and almost decided to just move on, to say a quick prayer, and introduce our night games. But I went ahead with the original plan and asked the leaders to spread out all over the room, and then I invited the youth to go to a leader and receive prayer. Immediately these teens got up out of their seats, started getting prayed for, and started praying for each other. There were tears all over the room and the Spirit of Jesus was palpable. I was shocked, but then again, I always seemed to be shocked and late to what God is actually doing. As I came down off of the stage, a line of teens were waiting to pray with me, and I took a mental note of their prayer requests:

> Youth 1: "I have regular anxiety attacks."
> Youth 2: "I think I might be gay."
> Youth 3: "I think I might gay."
> > (Youth 2 and Youth 3 don't know each other or each other's struggle)
> Youth 4: "I can't stop looking at porn."
> Youth 5: "I have never experienced peace, and I'm desperate for it."
> Youth 6: "My dad hasn't spoken to me in three months."

There were others, but you get the idea.

SO, WHERE'S YOUR FOCUS?

I belong to a few youth worker Facebook groups and, for the most part, I love the back and forth, the interactions, the support, the shared ideas, and the collaboration that's offered. But occasionally I see something I can't get my head around and I shout out at my screen, "What the heck are we doing?" It's like I'm reading posts from activity coordinators and Broadway show production departments.

Every once in a while, I see someone post their youth room's new stage and set design that goes with that month's theme. I see the pictures and, trust me, I know how much money, thought, and especially time it took to put that thing together. Honestly, it does nothing but frustrate me. Now don't get me wrong. I love visuals, set designs, and I love thematic teachings. So, I am a bit conflicted. I see the importance of creating an atmosphere that draws people into worship. I love that stuff. But (and this is a big BUT) when I see this focus on aesthetics in the context of what is happening culturally—all of these precious young people hurting and struggling, while God longs to bring them out of darkness and into his marvelous light—well, it all makes me wonder what in the world we are doing!

To me, all this other stuff is distracting us from what our calling really is about. And it's not that I think youth group shouldn't be fun or beautiful, in fact I think it should be the freest, most fun, creative place on earth. I just think we could be spending our money and time on more important things. Teens are super busy and super hurting, and we have to keep the main thing the main thing.

Years ago, I decided I wanted to take a percentage of our youth ministry's budget and resources and direct them outward. We would come alongside other organizations in the community in order to help them accomplish their dreams and goals:

schools, community centers, and after-school programs, like-minded parachurch organizations, etc. We'd be good news in the neighborhood. But that would mean no set designs and expensive short films to go with announcements or the sermon series. And what I ended up discovering is that it opened up doors to life with my teens. Instead of saying, "See you next week at youth group," I could say, "See you tomorrow at school." Why? Because I'd be there, helping to usher in light in a very dark place. Plus, I'd help the community as a whole understand where teens are and what they need. I'd be in a position to advocate, because I was all of a sudden a part of the systems they were living every day in.

In the last two weeks, I've picked up three students from school or met them at coffee shops. Every single teen, both public and private school attendees, spoke to me about how his or her school experience has been toxic, demanding, heavy, burdensome—you get it, right? Almost across the board, schools are extremely difficult places to be. These teens were struggling in debilitating places, like being at high altitude where the air is thin and you just can't seem to get enough oxygen in your lungs to breathe. I'm certain your youth feel very similar to mine.

So, what should we being doing?

How can we help?

How can we be a presence of hope in those places?

How can we play the vital role of advocacy?

Youth today are telling us some things, over and over and over again. We have to allow what they're saying to shape what our role might become.

First, they're telling us they feel alone. I hear it over and over again: "I feel completely alone, and no one is helping me, like, truly helping." They are in the midst of trying to figure themselves out and discover who they really are. But in an environment where mentoring and consistent adult investment is a lost art, this has become a nearly impossible task. It's no wonder adolescence has been extended to a fifteen- to twenty-year journey.

The things we have in place, like youth sports, the education system, the family, and even the church are no longer providing the support that's needed, but instead have become places of competition with unreasonable expectation. Even youth from families who don't have ridiculous expectations can't keep the pressure away from their own children, because it's just in the air and it's spreading like an air-born virus. Plus, when guidance counselors and teachers are pressured to get certain results on behalf of the school's funding and reputation, coaches are only about winning, and church leaders worry most about appearances and getting butts in seats, then our youth are grossly let down. They are feeling all alone as they navigate this not-so-easy world.

Second, they are telling us they are overwhelmed. I keep hearing it over and over again: "Brock, I'm just overwhelmed, and I can't seem to cope." Young people are overwhelmed by their families' brokenness and disconnection. They are overwhelmed by the pressure they feel from their schools, their teachers, and their coaches. Heck, they can even feel pressure from us, their youth leaders, to be good little boys and girls who never struggle or doubt and who hold on to their virginity like it is tied to their salvation. *Overwhelmed* is the right word. We know what it is to be overwhelmed. You know, you have all this pressure and all this work to do and all this expectation, but you can't see the forest for the trees. You don't know where to begin or how to think or what to feel. So, you just do your best to shut down your emotions and not think and just plow through it all, hoping at the end of the day you've landed where you're supposed to land.

And then connected to this is what I've been hearing in more recent years: "I feel like I have to be perfect and good at everything—*everything*, Brock. I'm overwhelmed with the pressure of being excellent at everything I do, and I fear people will discover I'm really not that good at any of it. And there is always room to do more, to be more, so I must. The pressure to be perfect is killing me."

And it's true, the systems in place make youth feel this way. With the pressure to maintain testing scores and get students into the "right" universities, our schools have become pressure cookers that demand students be excellent in every subject. And the very fact that students can take as many Advanced Placement courses as they want is ludicrous. Most of them are dying under the weight, but because they *can*, they must. And that is this generation's code: "If I can, then I should." It's a lie from the pit of hell. Just because you can do something *never* means you should. All of this is killing them. And it is so believed by them that as youth workers we can hardly get anywhere challenging it. Try to. See what happens. Kids believe this at their core, even if it's killing them.

And as youth workers we all know about the demands of sports. I could go on all day about this. The mass bowing down to the sports gods has given coaches way more power in the lives of young people than they've ever had in the past. Over the last ten years of ministry I have had youth, both male and female, come to camp with the stipulation that they complete their daily workout routines or they will not be allowed to play when they get back. And parents buy into this. Or worse, the youth don't come to camp at all because of their sixth-grade traveling soccer team.

The hard reality is that this pressure to be perfect can actually be more acute in the girls because of the added pressure to "be nice" all the time. This is often not an expectation, culturally, for the boys. Now, not all this pressure comes from home, as much of it is unspoken and exists within the larger culture. But this pressure to be perfect is creating youth who show up at church overwhelmed at the thought of school the next day.

"Brock, I just feel stuck, like there's no way out." This is what it's all leading to: stuckness. The systems in place seem inflexible and rigid with no hope of letting up. They feel stuck in their habits, with addiction occurring earlier and earlier, and stuck with all the pressure, with the ever-mounting sense of expectation and fear of letting people down. Many of their habits become respite from the pressure they feel, which creates, in turn, a nasty cycle. Guilt and shame follow them around and add to the pressure to hide their imperfections.

There's a hopelessness in the air. Recently I talked with a guy in our youth group who has been dealing with anxiety, and I asked him, "So, what can you do less of or stop doing altogether?"

He said, "Nothing. There's no way out, Brock. I just have to do it all." And then he said it: "Dude, I'm just stuck and there's no way out."

And all of this leads to the third thing I am hearing from our teens, which is connected to the first and the second: They are weighed down with shame. If you were reading between the lines of the others, you may have picked up on it. They feel utterly ashamed at their inability to overcome, to cope, to stop looking at porn, to stop questioning their faith, to not do the things they hate doing. Shame leads to hiding and hiding leads to a deeper level of pain and heartache and is debilitating. Both teens who confessed their sexual confusion had been struggling with it for several years in secret. I was the first person either one had ever told.

Sometimes the way we live out our theology can lead to legalism. When the goal is to "be perfect," things in our lives that don't line up are hidden away; they become secret sins. When we don't have a safe place to take our shame, it grows.

And, if you've been in youth ministry for any length of time, these are probably things you already know. But I needed to set the table, because God is longing to raise up youth workers who don't just provide a space one night a week for teens to escape from their pain. God is longing to raise up people who will strive to be culture changers and advocates for these precious ones.

The reason why we have jobs in youth ministry is because the church woke up, because historically the church had no clue what to do with teens. But now the church has become aware of the need to reach and care for youth, especially since the other traditional systems are failing them. The church just doesn't know how to do it. So, for me the big question is how are we, as youth workers, going to truly make a difference in the communities God has placed us in?

REINVENTING OUR ROLES

I was talking with Adam McLane recently on the phone. He's a partner at The Youth Cartel and a legend when it comes to youth ministry advocacy. Adam shares my annoyance with set designs and expensive lighting at youth group, especially when it gets in the way of truly caring for the hearts, minds, and souls of youth. But he said a couple of really important things I believe can shape our view of advocacy.

Adam recently ran for a seat on his neighborhood council and actually won. He is now officially advocating for a better community for his youth to live and grow up in. This is exactly what we, as youth workers, should be about.

First, Adam said, we must see ourselves as youth advocates in our cities and communities. Youth workers today cannot see themselves as only program directors, Bible teachers, or even small group leaders. Instead, we have to reinvent ourselves as the voice that advocates for the youth of the community to the community. Think about it. Who else is doing it? Why are teens stuck? Why do they have no power? Hardly anyone is speaking up for them or even empowering them to speak up for themselves.

Secondly, Adam said that you can't Lone Ranger it. Youth workers today have to acknowledge there are other people in the community, no matter how few, who actually do care about youth today and are giving their lives for them. And so we must collaborate with school guidance counselors, teachers, principals, after-school coordinators, and headmasters. But we must also partner with the city council, the school board, and the mayor's office. People in the faith and outside of it, and we must see and understand that all of us are on the same team. This means we're going to the local school board meetings and we're at every city meeting where the needs of community youth are being addressed.

It's just my belief that being present and giving time to meetings like these will be much more effective in the long run than designing your next thematic set or spending hours editing a video you could have empowered a teen to edit. I think we need to work smarter not harder. But this is also going to mean carrying the vision of advocacy in the community to our pastors and supervisors. They have to get it. They have to understand what the battle is and what is at stake and, my friends, that is going to take hard work and time to bring systemic change to the places that are causing damage among our youth.

I actually had a great example of this in my very first youth ministry position in Glendale, California. My supervisor was a vital part of the community; he had relationships with the police department, the mayor, the school boards. He was their first call when a crisis hit and their first call when they wanted to help teens. I have attempted to model my ministry after this first experience, realizing that reaching a city with the really good news of the gospel is done much better when we rally together around a shared cause: our youth. The ensuing partnerships, relationships, and mutual respect will even open people up to our churches and to hearing our stories.

But there are lies we have to expose, and they are…

> "Every student has to go to college or they're a failure."
> "Busy teens are happy teens and out-of-trouble teens."
> "Straight A's mean a teen is doing great in life."
> "The only way to challenge smart young people is to have them take AP courses."
> "The American dream leads to happiness." ("Take the right classes, get the right grades, get into the right college, get the right job that pays the right amount, so you can live a comfortable life one day..." The American dream is robbing from the kingdom dream).

My wife Kelsey was reading an article about valedictorians. In the article, it said the people who become difference-makers many times are the rule-breakers and the so-called "failures" who never give up. These are the youth who have a difficult start in life, and they're rough around the edges. What is also interesting is that the valedictorians many times are actually the in-the-box thinkers, the rule-followers, the line-walkers, and the insiders. The article showed that most valedictorians don't turn out to be big difference-makers as adults.

I find that interesting because we've defined success for students as something that may not actually get them to where they want to be or even what we need as a society. We might even dismiss and not see the potential in the youth who just don't fit. And I mean this culturally. It's amazing to me how those who might grow up to be difference-makers many times get off to a rough start; and then over time and as they gather more and more wisdom because of not-so-good choices, they end up learning when rules should be broken. And friends, there are times when rules should be broken. When these teens get out of the box and see everything from a different perspective, they can begin to expose the lies that are damaging.

In the mid-1980s, my dad was a youth pastor and was considering taking a job in Northern California. Now the head pastor of the church we were at had been fired and the place was in disarray. My dad felt he had done his time there and the church just really needed a clean and fresh start. One day he was sitting in his home office and the phone rang. It was a man who said he had been saved at a concert from back in the day when my parents were in their Christian rock band. But the man said this, "Paul, I am a pastor now, and I was doing my devotions and felt like God wanted me to tell you something. I'm not sure even what you're doing these days or what is going on, but God wants you to know you're like Nehemiah where you are. God is calling you to stay there and head back into the ditches and grab the old stones and rebuild the walls with what is already there. Rebuild the walls, Paul, and God will bless the work of your hands. He will protect you."

Well that's all my dad needed to hear. We stayed, he became the head pastor to those hurting and broken people, and together they rebuilt the walls of that church.

There is a high school guy in our group who really struggles with all kinds of fears. He is currently an eleventh grader, and at times his fears have been debilitating. Recently I got an idea. What if he started helping me help others? In fact, what if we took all of these struggling youth and allowed their pain to be used *now*? What if we headed back into the ditch and grabbed what was there, in the midst of all the mess and dirt, and allowed God to use it to build other teens' lives?

This began a chain reaction, and what I noticed is that our youth have begun to be hope-carriers to their peers. This one guy, in particular, has found his mission, his life calling; and it has begun for him now. He's a co-laborer with us. Youth *helping us* expose the lies and *helping us* advocate for a better system just might be the way forward. I don't know, I just sense a movement on the horizon.

Don't you know that you yourselves are God's temple
and that God's Spirit dwells in your midst?
– Paul of Tarsus
1 Corinthians 3:16 (NLT)

CHAPTER 6
THAT OTHER PERSON

S o, I'm about to confess to you something I've never told anyone. Okay, well, that's really not true, but I've not told anyone who isn't a really close friend, for fear of being theologically banished. I speak and minister to all types of churches and theological systems and traditions, so I've learned to keep some things to myself. But here it is: When I was in elementary school, I spoke in tongues.

I know what you might be thinking. Either you're disturbed by that and thinking, "Ha, I knew he was a secret charismatic. I'm done reading this book." Or, you're pleasantly surprised because maybe you identify as charismatic and you're way into that other person we call the Holy Spirit. But to be honest, I think it would be easiest for me to just tell you the story before we get into any theological implications.

Back when I was a little kid my family went to a Sunday evening service. This was in the days when the whole family would go to two services on Sundays, one in the morning and one in the evening. The best part of the Sunday evening service was when it was over, because afterward we'd all head out to eat pizza at Mr. Ghatti's Pizza Parlor.

But at this one particular Sunday evening service, all of the parents were supposed to bring their children, and there was going to be a time when the prayer team at the church was going to pray for each child individually. I honestly don't remember much about that evening except for this: Someone prayed for me. I don't remember who, but when they did I started speaking in another language. As I was quietly speaking, a woman came running over and started crying out and telling everyone that I was speaking in her home country's language. She said I was declaring the good news of Jesus.

Now, I don't know what your theology says about that. You might be a skeptic like I have often been and think the whole thing was a manipulation of a little boy. But I have to tell you something: For me, it was real. I clearly remember sensing God's presence in a life-altering kind of way, but I don't remember what I said or how I said it. But then that was it, it was over.

Years went by and after that experience I saw a lot of fake and manipulative things within some of the charismatic churches my parents were attending and a part of for a while. It put a bad taste in my mouth about all things Holy Spirit. Typically what we do, and what I did, is to move to the opposite extreme of whatever disillusions us. But life isn't black and white, in fact many times it's grey. Truth tends to be somewhere in the middle, but I moved clear to the other side theologically.

In fact, when I decided I wanted to attend a Christian college to study theology, I made sure it was a school that wasn't charismatic. After four years of studying there I went and did a biblical studies program for a year at a similar place, and then after that I went to a dispensational seminary. If you're not sure what dispensationalism is, it's a big system of theology that basically says God works in different ways according to the time. It follows that one of the important distinctions of dispensationalism is the belief that the gifts of the Holy Spirit have passed away, are no longer in play, and now we're in a different dispensation of time. We don't really need that gift anymore, those who follow this theology would say, we have the Scriptures now.

Many years later I was visiting my parents and sitting in the pew listening to my father speak. He was a pastor at that time in Oregon, and the funny thing is, I don't even remember what he was talking about. (But it obviously wasn't about sex. I would have remembered a talk about sex. But that's neither here nor there.) What I remember is sitting there with this feeling. See, I knew I was missing something from my life. Now don't get me wrong, I did sense God's presence in my life at the time. I felt his power, and it's important to know that just because people don't believe in the gifts of the Spirit, it doesn't mean they don't sense his presence. But in that moment, I knew I had been limiting the Lord in my own life and in the way I was leading youth. I didn't want to move back toward some of the extremism I'd seen in certain churches, but I also knew I needed to be more biblical in how I perceived and experienced the Holy Spirit.

See, just like my youth, I was longing for a God who was real and worked and would fill me with love, joy, peace, forbearance, kindness, goodness, faithfulness, gentleness, and self-control. I was desperate for this new in-filling; and my youth, who were living in this high-paced, high-anxiety life, with little—if any at all—peace, needed a new work of God in their lives. I sat there and just repented. I knew I needed a mind change, a direction change; and I knew the way I was leading my ministry was in need of some tweaking.

So, the first step in opening my own life up to Christ's Spirit was to ask him to empower me daily. I prayed every day for him to strengthen me, fill me, and then I even told him that if he wanted me to speak in tongues again, I'd be open to it. (As long as it wasn't weird. Please, no weird!)

I prayed this prayer for a solid year, every single day. (Now again, I realize I may be in hot water with some of you right now. But honestly, I don't mind.) Do know that I'm actually more concerned with every believer being filled with the *fruit* of the Spirit than speaking in tongues. But because of my story and that early childhood experience, I just felt like I needed some confirmation. I needed to know if it was real or not. So, every day I prayed that prayer, and then about year later I was standing in a church service in London. Tim Hughes was leading us in worship, and I was—along with a couple thousand other people—singing from my guts, declaring the goodness of God. All of a sudden, I started to speak in another language. Right there in the midst of this loud worship was me, speaking just like I had as a little boy.

No one touched me or laid their hands on me, and no one (including me) was acting "weird." In fact, no one even noticed. But afterwards I gathered a few of my friends who were there with me and told them. They all knew that I had been praying every day for a year, and we just huddled up and laughed and cried together. Again, this isn't something I fully get, and it wasn't something I even implemented into my ministry back home. But it was an experience that built my faith and my trust, and it made me bold and gave me the courage to invite the Holy Spirit back into my ministry with youth.

Now let me just pause for a second, because I know I've probably lost some of you with this chapter. But if you're still tracking with me or still curious, let's bring this all back to the teens we're encountering today.

They are desperate for a God who is real. In fact, we all are. To summarize everything you read in the last chapter: They're over-scheduled, full of fears, anxieties, addictions, and OCD behaviors. Many are on medications, and they're just trying to make it through the middle school and high school years, hoping college will at least give them the freedom and peace they long for. Let me use that word again—they are *desperate*.

The problem is most teens go to youth groups that do

announcements longer than they pray. Most are a part of youth ministries whose youth pastors entertain them with dynamic storytelling and lead them in a couple of games and then send these desperate youth on their way. Maybe after a talk they get to jump into small groups where at least they can experience intimacy with some of their peers and possibly a caring adult, but intimacy with God eludes them for the bulk of their teenage experience.

For me, after that night in London, I knew I needed to change the way I was leading. I needed to be a true biblical Trinitarian and invite my youth to join me in living out the whole of the gospel. I flew back home, but I wasn't sure how to proceed.

MAKING ROOM FOR THE HOLY SPIRIT

A few weeks later I was in Oklahoma speaking at a state Nazarene camp and sensed God leading me to try something. Now, typically I can move an audience, and I rely on that ability to get a response from youth. I (like many of you) try to share the whole of the gospel with them and then (depending on the camp) might ask them to come forward for prayer or maybe to turn to their leaders for prayer. But I love to at least give an opportunity for youth to respond to what God might be doing in the moment. And in my prayer time before I spoke, I sensed God tell me to just talk about the fruit of the Spirit and then ask them to stand and, in silence, ask God to fill them with whatever it was that they needed. This may not sound like a big deal to you, but for me it was huge. So, I went up and talked about how God's Spirit was longing to empower them and give them the peace and the hope and the self-control that they were desperate for. (There's that word again: *desperate*.) Then I just asked everyone, a couple thousand of them, to stand with their palms up and open and ask God to fill them. Then I just quietly stood there.

Maybe you're like me and you hate silence. It can be really awkward. Especially silence that lasts way too long and makes the room feel uncomfortable. My tendency is to let the audience be still and sit in the silence for a minute, maybe two, at most. But then I usually want them to move, to receive prayer, or just want to have the worship band come up and lead a song or two of response. Quiet feels dangerous and scary to me. I feel out of control. But I really wanted to be obedient to the Lord. So, I just stood there with all these amazing teens in the silence and waited. We waited, standing in the silence for about five minutes. No word was spoken, and all of a sudden it happened. God started quietly working. These young people started coming to the front to pray, on their knees. Teens everywhere were crying and praying for each other. I stood there amazed by what I was seeing. I didn't generate a thing. I didn't manipulate or cause anything, not a thing. We simply together asked God's Spirit to work.

The next morning the camp had teens share about what God had done in their lives that weekend. In story after story, they shared about how they didn't believe, were full of doubt or hurt, or were lacking peace in their lives; but when they asked God's Spirit to fill them, they truly received something that was unexpected. They weren't moved by their own brokenness. They were moved because they really believed they had encountered God himself.

No one even mentioned me. (Ouch.) All they could talk about was how they initially stood in doubt and only begrudgingly invited God's Spirit to do a work. And then to their surprise, he had. And here's the awesome thing: It felt like it was supposed to feel. God was doing the work himself. I just needed to set the stage and allow him to do what he does best.

It was what I had been missing in my ministry.

It wasn't weird. It wasn't a "charismatic" experience. It wasn't Pentecostal "mumbo-jumbo." It was Christianity. And it changed everything for me. And I went home with the courage to make some changes. To make space for God to work in the lives of my youth. And what happened was that my little struggling youth group exploded. God started working every week. They actually started inviting their friends, which was a huge surprise, and suddenly we had a little movement on our hands.

Years later, I now find myself at a new church in a very different environment. A few months ago, I took a job overseeing a large youth ministry in a church just outside of Washington DC. It's full of "good kids," many of whom are from very "religious" homes. It's a strong Bible-teaching youth ministry but, like my previous ministry, it was lacking openness to God's Spirit. So, a few weeks ago we got to take these amazing youth away for my first retreat with them. The problem is that they didn't really know me yet and were still a bit skeptical about this West Coast youth pastor. So, I felt afraid to lead them in the way I've grown accustomed to in recent years.

But Saturday night came, which—as we've noted—is when Jesus is traditionally scheduled to show up. I finished my gospely talk (is "gospely" a word? eh, who cares) and then I tried it again. I stood there on the stage, under the lights, and simply said, "Hey, let's stand together and just ask God to work in our lives. To empower us and give us peace or joy or whatever it is you're desperate for."

They all stood up, and after a few moments in silence, God began to do what he does best when we give him room and space to do so. No one was shaking or barking like a dog. No one had a strange hairdo or wore weird makeup like some televangelist. These were just a bunch of kids and adults desperate for the in-breaking Spirit of God to work. And he did. I just needed to create space for him to give us what each one of us needed. It makes me wonder if there is even space or room for God anymore in our services.

I love Francis Chan, and in the book *Forgotten God*, he said:

> "I'm willing to bet there are millions of churchgoers across America who cannot confidently say that they have experienced his presence or action in their lives over the past year. And many of them do not believe they can. The benchmark of success in church services has become more about attendance than the movement of the Holy Spirit. The 'entertainment' model of church was largely adopted in the 1980s and '90s and while it alleviated some of our boredom for a couple of hours a week, it filled our churches with self-focused consumers rather than self-sacrificing servants attuned to the Holy Spirit... The light of the American church is flickering and nearly extinguished, having largely sold out to the kingdoms and values of this world... We are not all we were made to be when everything in our lives and churches can be explained apart from the work and presence of the Spirit of God... Shouldn't there be a huge difference between the person who has the Spirit of God living inside of him or her and the person who does not?"[6]

I'm with Chan. There was something missing from my life and from the lives of the youth I was ministering to. I'm just really longing for a movement, and honestly, I don't believe we will see it unless the universal church re-embraces God's Spirit with wide openness. Do it within your own theological understandings, but for goodness' sake, do it. Teach your youth to understand how to be still, to wait upon the Lord. The Scriptures tell us that if we wait on him, then he will renew our strength. We will actually walk and not faint (Isaiah 40:31).

Well, we've been seeing a lot of teens completely stop the walking, and they have no strength to withstand culture's pull. What if we taught them how to wait upon the Lord? What if we preached what it meant to be daily surrendered to his leading and empowerment? Maybe then—with God's Spirit at work in our ministries, in our lives, and in the lives of our youth—we wouldn't have to waste so much time with all the nonsense. We could create an environment where teens would not only sense God's warmth but learn how to be filled with his power and with his strength. They are desperate for that, and so are we.

RADICAL COMMITMENT

I started out in youth ministry in Young Life. The goal then was to, through an incarnational ministry approach, simply introduce teenagers to Jesus through a relationship with them on their own turf. We spoke to them and tried to help them just have a relationship with Christ. But never did we speak about God's Spirit, not even with our campaigner youth. What we were doing, really, was teaching them how to have a relationship with God that mostly led to a head-knowledge kind of faith. The problem is that it's impossible to have a living and breathing relationship with God without his Spirit.

Now the Young Life model, whether you know it or not, is what has swept the nation for the past forty years, as far as strategies and ministry models and structures. They did and are doing a heck of a lot for us that is positive. Just the concept of being Jesus in the world of young people was a game-changer for youth ministry around the globe. But we've stayed there and kind of focused on right thinking, proper theology, and a head-knowledge kind of religion. But if you look at every movement of God *en masse*, the Holy Spirit was at the forefront. In fact, each movement was marked by two things: passionate prayer and a radical commitment to holiness.

This is what we have to do, but it first begins with us. Daily passionate prayer. Daily radical commitment to holiness. And it can actually start with just a few of us. I'm in. I'm ready.

I love Eugene Peterson. I love his writings—not just *The Message Bible*, but it's brilliant. So, I want to end this chapter with a passage:

> *But if God himself has taken up residence in your life, you can hardly be thinking more of yourself than of him. Anyone, of course, who has not welcomed this invisible but clearly present God, the Spirit of Christ, won't know what we're talking about.*
> *But for you who welcome him, in whom he dwells— even though you still experience all the limitations of sin—you yourself experience life on God's terms. It stands to reason, doesn't it, that if the alive-and-present God who raised Jesus from the dead moves into your life, he'll do the same thing in you that he did in Jesus, bringing you alive to himself? When God lives and breathes in you (and he does, as surely as he did in Jesus), you are delivered from that dead life. With his Spirit living in you, your body will be as alive as Christ's!*
> *So don't you see that we don't owe this old do-it-yourself life one red cent. There's nothing in it for us, nothing at all. The best thing to do is give it a decent burial and get on with your new life. God's Spirit beckons. There are things to do and places to go!*
> *This resurrection life you received from God is not a timid, grave-tending life. It's adventurously expectant, greeting God with a childlike "What's next, Papa?" God's Spirit touches our spirits and confirms who we really are. We know who he is, and we know who we are: Father and children. And we know we are going to get what's coming to us—an unbelievable*

inheritance! We go through exactly what Christ goes through. If we go through the hard times with him, then we're certainly going to go through the good times with him!
– Romans 8:9-17 (MSG)

Why fit in, when you were born to stand out?
– Dr. Seuss

CHAPTER 7
THE BIG MOVE: FROM YOUTH MINISTRY TO YOUTH IN MINISTRY

Have you ever wondered why Jesus didn't go to the Pharisees and convince them that he was the Messiah? If you think about it, that would have been a much better strategy. Go to the church leaders and open the Scriptures and slowly reveal to them who you are and what the plan is. I can see it now: They come out of the temple on fire, ready to be a part of ushering in a new revelation and mission of bringing love and forgiveness and hope to the world. I know what you might be thinking, and there were definitely reasons why this wasn't the method Jesus used—one being that the Pharisees were a bunch jerks.

But here's the deal, the church was not the place for God to work. The church people of that day were consumed with behavior, not the hearts of people. They were consumed with attendance, not community change. They were concerned with dollars and budget, not renewal. They wanted control and power, not freedom and personal liberation. The church just wasn't trustworthy enough to have their hands on the movement. It would have ended before it began.

God's Spirit left the temple 400 years before Jesus even showed up on the scene. The church was just a dead, empty building. Now I know the whole topic is much more nuanced and complex than my silly thoughts and questions, but the point is clear: God needed to move past the religious systems and institutions of the day to usher in something new. Sometimes it's just easier to launch a brand-new initiative with young, hungry, daring, and wide-open hearts and minds. We were eating dinner with friends who recently made a choice to stop going to church. We really love being with them, and the funny thing is that we completely get why they left. But it's not just them. Thousands in America are walking out the door, swearing never to return. In the opening of the book *Why Nobody Wants to Go to Church Anymore*, Thom and Joani Schultz ask these provocative questions, paraphrased here:

- Even though more than 90% of Americans say they believe in God, why did most of them avoid church last weekend?
- Why are nearly one in five Americans checking "none" for their religious affiliation—the fastest growing, highest-ever documented segment?
- Why are researchers predicting that by 2020 more than 85% of Americans won't worship God at church?
- If 88% of adults say their faith is important to them, why do the majority of them choose not to grow their faith in church?
- Why are nearly two-thirds (64%) open to pursuing their faith in an environment that's different from a typical church?
- Last weekend most people in America avoided church. And a sizable portion who did make it to church wished they were somewhere else. Why?[7]

Well similar things are happening across American youth groups. It's a multi-generational thing here in the States. It's not just that churches are shrinking, but youth ministries are not what they used to be. The numbers are going down and teens are finding other ways to spend their time. But I wonder if it's all connected. If it's not just a young adult thing or a kid thing, but a human thing. Everyone is having the same thoughts and feelings, and it's this: They are just not seeing the need for church, and they're demonstrating it by not showing up anymore, with no regrets and maybe for good reason.

I had coffee yesterday with a lead pastor at a mega-church.

This church he's been pastoring for many years is now seeing their attendance quickly dwindle. So, this nationally prominent and influential church is struggling. He told me he hasn't been sleeping and he can't figure out what the deal is. But this is happening, and it's not just in this pastor's church. It's all over the place.

My friends who we were having dinner with, who left the church, said they just couldn't do it anymore. For them it was more than the typical reasons—too judgmental, too business-oriented, no Spirit, too safe and palatable. No, they were just sick of the show.

But people show up for a good show, right? I mean dynamic worship and great teaching is what leads us to a growing congregation, right?

Nope. Today, people are longing for transcendence. In other words, they're longing to be participants in something greater than themselves. They are dying for a life worth living, but they show up and all they see is an inauthentic show. They're just sick of it. It's too polished, too slick, too professional, and too observational. People want to get some skin in the game, especially the young.

This is why I believe the next movement will start with the young, because there is this fire that burns inside them, longing to run, ready to be set in motion. They sign up to follow Jesus wherever he calls them, but then they're told to just be quiet and sit in rows and watch the professionals do it.

I wonder if it's all a stench to the Lord?

EMPOWERING AND RELEASING YOUTH
As a youth pastor over the years, one of my favorite things

has been to watch students perform at their schools—plays, sporting events, recitals, concerts, and whatever else they happen to be involved in. I've even been known to jump into a classroom to watch a student give a speech. I absolutely love it. I love sitting with the students' parents and their friends, and together we just cheer them on. But almost every time I leave the school with a haunting thought: Hardly anyone ever comes to youth group to watch teens do anything.

But the reason for that is obvious: *Teens are hardly ever doing anything at youth group.*

A main reason why many of us got into youth work to begin with was we actually believe in youth. Like all great teachers, we think young people can do amazing things. As a youth pastor, I started taking my cue from the schools I was visiting. I stopped giving talks by myself. I started having the youth lead or co-lead the worship, having them pray for their friends during ministry time, and basically running everything we did. I started seeing myself more as a developer and a mentor and an empowerer of young people.

I never went to a school to watch the adults in charge perform—not once. The adults were always behind the scenes, empowering and releasing students to do what they do best. After watching those educators for years, I knew I had to get off the stage and truly start empowering teens, developing teens. I honestly think that is why youth are struggling today with church and with faith. They never found a place or a role for themselves within the church—a place where they could really dive in, use their gifts, be a part of something bigger than themselves, and soar. Like I said, teenagers today are longing for transcendence; they truly want to contribute to something that is larger than themselves.

Now, youth ministry has done a decent job at getting teens in the worship band, but for the most part, American youth go to church to watch the adults in charge do their thing. And then we wonder why we see little engagement, little growth, and not much sustainability.

It's actually quite funny or maybe just sad: We leave youth group and we ask our spouse or friends, "So, was my talk okay, did I do alright?" Then they affirm us and we feel good about ourselves. But to me this seems backwards and just plain ridiculous and really embarrassing. It's also typical of adults. In fact when you look at it, most things in the country that were once put in place for youth have been reversed and now have become about the adults in charge. We're good at making things about us, aren't we? (See Chap Clark's book, *Hurt: Inside the World of Today's Teenagers* [Baker, 2004], for more on this.)

Now, it's not that we haven't done youth development. Every spring and summer, all around the country, youth groups are on mission trips. Teens are living the way of Jesus, contributing, using their gifts. And they are coming to life because of it. They actually have a role to play, they are engaged, and are finally doing it. But then we go back home to the same systems that squash everything we put in place on the mission. (Ugh.)

Many of us are longing to see a change. We want to see a movement happen in youth ministry—where youth ministry is about youth development, discipleship, investment, and commissioning. I'm hoping that youth work actually becomes *youth at work*—or as my friend Timothy Eldred says, "We have to move from youth ministry to youth in ministry." That is, youth doing the work, being equipped and empowered to use their gifts and abilities. (More about Tim in just a moment.)

A lot has been said about and written about the topic of student leadership. Yet, in my opinion, it's one of the biggest struggles in youth ministry. There are systemic issues that have kept us from actually seeing great student leadership happen. Maybe it's because we treat it like an add-on. We have our weekly youth group meetings, weekly small groups, and monthly activities, followed by retreats, camps, and mission trips— leaving very little room to also throw into the mix a student leadership program. Many have tried to do it, and what began with great excitement, fizzled out as roadblocks popped up.

So, what do we do?

First, I had a conversation with Tim Eldred about this, and it was so rich I wanted to include it here. Just so you know who he is, Tim has been the president over at Endeavor Ministries since 2005. It's the oldest youth ministry organization in the world, and he has a wealth of knowledge.

I hope you enjoy our conversation:

Me: Tim, you've been preaching for "youth ministry" to make a move to "youth *in* ministry" for so many years. Why are you so passionate about this?

Tim: Names matter, Brock. What we call something is typically what it becomes. God gave us that ability in Genesis, and it's still true today. When we started referring to youth work as "youth ministry" only a few decades ago, we inadvertently robbed it of its original intent to train youth *in* ministry. We also removed another critical component of youth work: We removed the apostrophe. Long before you and I entered youth work, it was referred to as "youth's ministry" or "young people's work." I'm passionate to return to the roots of youth work, when young people had ownership and possession of their faith and adults were supports and advocates who helped youth do ministry, not do it for them. Why? Because historically, that's when we saw the greatest spiritual growth in young people.

Me: I love this and I love the bigger story of Endeavor Ministries and what you're trying to do. Can you give me the thirty-second version of the grand story and mission?

Tim: Sure. Here's my elevator pitch. In 1881, there was a pastor named Dr. Francis Clark in Portland, Maine. He was dealing with the same issue you and I struggle with today: The large majority of young people were leaving the church or abandoning their faith as they entered adulthood. In a bold move, he prayerfully decided to take a risk and raise the bar in hopes they would respond to higher expectations and greater accountability. (By the way, that's exactly what our current generation is asking for from the church now.) So, on a Sunday afternoon in February, Clark invited fifty-seven young people between the ages of ten and eighteen to his home and he made two statements:

1. "I believe young people can make the same level of commitment to Jesus Christ as adults."
2. "I promise to never do anything for you in the church you can learn to do yourselves."

He then defined the outcomes—the what and why. Then he gave them permission to design the outputs—the how, when, where, and who. He supported *their* ministry. The entire experience was an opportunity to learn by doing. The youth movement that emerged became a training school of the church for youth *in* ministry. And through the leadership of young people with the hands-off guidance of a handful of adults, Christian Endeavor swelled in ranks and swept the globe, growing to over four million youth in 67,000 churches in only a few years.

Young people were empowered to risk failure and make mistakes to do something for Jesus. They weren't expected to be flawless. They were experiencing God working through

113

their lives as they were training for mission and ministry. But the key was they always had ownership; the apostrophe mattered. It still does, more than we realize.

Me: We've clearly swayed away from this mindset. So, how do we make this move to youth in ministry again?

Tim: First, we have to return to the idea that originally gave birth to youth work before we called it youth ministry. Nothing changes for us until we can embrace this principle, "Never do anything in the church for young people that they can learn to do themselves." It's a mindset, Brock. Not another method or model. Once we change our minds, everything else follows suit without forcing it.

Second, we have to redefine the role of adults in youth work. The responsibility of vocational and volunteer youth workers can be explained with three words: model, mentor, and mobilize. Notice I didn't say plan, program, and present. That equation won't produce youth in ministry. We've proven that quite well in the last few years.

Third, we must create a safe space and place where young people can risk failure for what breaks their hearts. Where they can once again learn by doing. The role can also be redefined in three words: discover, develop, and deploy. When we stop giving answers and start asking better questions, youth are allowed to dream and express their fears and their faith in an environment where it's okay to try new things and find out what they're capable of doing and how God can use them for his purpose today—not someday.

Me: As you know, I'm absolutely convinced this is the way forward, but let's get practical for a moment. How do we do this when teens have very little time, are stressed and over-scheduled, and barely show up now as it is?

Tim: We start with their hearts. We've been so busy telling young people what to think and believe that maybe we've failed to find out what's really important to them. Here's my favorite dialogue to have with a student. "So, what breaks your heart?" And then I shut up and wait.

Most of the time their answer is, "I don't know." And when I ask them why not, their answer is usually, "Because no one has ever asked me before. I've never really thought about it much."

With a little persistence and an authentic desire to hear their heart, I just keep asking while praying that God would break their heart with a need, issue, or cause. Eventually, they will answer with a problem they'd like to solve. When they do, I ask another question. "So, what would you do about that if nothing were standing in your way?"

Again, their response most of the time is, "I don't know. No one's ever asked me that before." So, I keep asking and praying until they say, "I've got an idea about how to fix that problem."

My reply, "So, how can I help you?"

Our job is to help youth do ministry, not do ministry for youth. Practically, we become advisors and set them up for success. We don't take over and plan a program around their heartbeat. They are the program. We help them make decisions by asking more questions like,

> "So, what does the Bible say about that need?"
> "So, do you have friends with the same passion who
>   could help you?"
> "So, what are you lacking to get the job done?"
> "So, do you know an adult you trust who could mentor
>   you in your mission?"

It's literally that simple, Brock. But let me warn you that this is the hardest youth work you'll ever do. Youth in ministry takes more time and energy that youth ministry, but it produces the results we all dream of for the next generation.[8]

I love what Tim shared. So, let's end this chapter with this. Here are what I believe to be some keys to a great youth development program. But I offer them with a warning: *They might get you fired.*

Step 1: Begin by killing all your programs.
Step 2: Let the youth rebuild the ministry.
Step 3: Give them the keys to drive what's developed.
Step 4: Put youth on teams with adult point people to run the new ministry. (Adults as point people is vital to discipleship and sustainability.)
Step 5: Your role becomes instigator, listener, empowerer, pursuer of teens, and the great encourager.
Step 6: Let them, and it, fail.
Step 7: Make student leadership meetings become first priority for the ministry.
Step 8: Never do a solo-anything again—even tag-team talks with teens.
Step 9: Embrace the messy.
Step 10: Watch and enjoy exponential growth in the lives of your youth.

Life's full of lots of dream-stealers always telling you, you need to do something more sensible. I think it doesn't matter what your dream is, just fight the dream-stealers and hold on to it.
– Bear Grylls

CHAPTER 8
THE DEBILITATING PRESENCE:
MODALITY VS. SODALITY

We were sitting in a circle in the living room; all of us were pastors. It was truly a holy moment. And with a deep breath he said, "I just want to minister without fear, you know what I mean? I'm tired of being afraid. Afraid of people, afraid of losing my job, afraid of speaking truth. I want to be in a church that's committed to a generous orthodoxy, that's full of love and grace, and that allows people to journey. I'm tired of this pit in my stomach. I'm tired of church not being safe. I'm just tired."

We all resonated and quietly nodded our heads in agreement.

A few years ago, I looked at my wife and said, "I just can't do it anymore. I don't think I can work in the church one more day." I had been going to work with that same pit in my stomach for about a year. Anxiety was ever present, and I'd wake up each morning and head into my office, close the door, and hide. I hated it. I was tired of feeling alone, not supported, afraid of losing my job. The weight of the whole thing was killing me. Really, I was way too tired, not in a good place, and a bit paranoid. But also, the church I was working in was a toxic dog-eat-dog battleground. And I was tired of seeing the good guys shoot the good guys. The church has always had a problem with in-fighting. I mean, just read the New Testament. I just wanted us to shoot some bad guys for once, if only we could agree on who that really was.

When I first went into ministry, I had such high hopes of what it would be like to work in a church. Funny thing was, I should have known better. After all, I am a pastor's kid. Heck, I'm the grandkid of pastors as well, on both sides. That's three generations of pastors, and every single generation has been devastatingly hurt by the church they were serving in. Why was I so naïve?

My grandfather was working in a church and was having tremendous success reaching the community. But he ended up getting fired and thrown out because of the type of people he was reaching. The lack of vision and radical self-centeredness of that church and that denomination is one of many tragic experiences in our family.

My parents have been hurt in every single church they have ever ministered in. They'd go many years with amazing success, but it would never end well. I don't tell you this because I want you to quit on the church or, if you're considering ministry, not to. But there's a definite problem in the church today. Heck, there's been a problem for generations. In many cases, as you may know, it's just not a safe place—and not just for pastors ministering in the church. And we wonder why Millennials are walking away. There's a sickness inside those doors.

I was having coffee with a parishioner of a different church in our city, and he began complaining about their youth pastor and how he couldn't seem to get teens to show up regularly, especially during the spring semester. He said this youth pastor is never in the office and he just goes and watches youth at their games and performances. He said it like this youth pastor was Mr. Slacker.

"What?" I exclaimed. "You mean you have a youth pastor who understands teens are over-scheduled and can't always make it out to the church's youth services, so he's taking the time in the evenings and on the weekends to go to where they are? You're nuts! You should be throwing a parade in his honor. You should give him a raise. You should bring him in front of the whole church and celebrate that he's not in the office but on the front lines and in the world where kids are living."

I'm amazed at how many in the church just don't get it.

So, one night I was complaining to my wife about how the church seemed at odds with itself. Now, my wife is finishing up her MDiv, and in one of her classes they had been studying about the two main structures that make up the church called the *sodality* and the *modality*, terms explored by Ralph Winter in the brilliant book, *Perspectives on the World Christian Movement*.[9] I know these words might be strange or foreign to some, but they just might be one of the secrets to some of the mess we find ourselves in.

But to be specific, the *modality* is the static or geographical form of the church—the church as a local or regional community. The *sodality* is the mobile or missional form of the church—the church as a specialist or missional agency.

Now, if we're not careful, these two critical parts of the church can be at odds with each other and really can have a hard time coexisting. The modality is the organizational structure set in place to keep the church stable and consistent, and the modality sets up systems and processes to do so. It is the "sending" part of the church that flourishes when it uses its resources to extend God's kingdom.

But then there's the part of the church called the sodality, the "sent" arm, which is always longing to reach higher. Fueled by a white-hot faith, a discontent with the status quo, a sense that God is calling them to more, and a vision for a particular mission. The sodality is usually filled to excess with vision, energy, and giftings, but never seems to have enough money to make it all happen. Youth ministry easily and naturally falls into this category. Youth ministry, as the sodality, is on the front lines in the midst of culture, helping young people navigate and discover truth in their own context, always pointing them to Jesus and pushing the envelope to reach more.

So, to be even more clear, the modality contains the HR department, the established format, and usually the wallet; but it also functions in a community as a hub out of which ministry is birthed and people are cared for. The sodality is the mission, the going, the outward face—such as community VBS, campus ministry, and all missional endeavors to reach into the community at large where they are at.

Now historically, as I said, youth ministry has fit nicely into the passionate sodality stream, the missional agency of the church. The church wants the youth ministry to reach the local schools, to draw youth in, to grow, and to empower the church kids to invite friends. It's about calling teens to join them in making a difference for the sake of the gospel. But the tension comes when we, as the sodality, forget that there are some aspects of modality to our jobs and the church forgets that a major part of our role is to be the out there, not in the office.

THE TENSION

I've recently experienced this firsthand in my new church. Right away I saw a collision between the modality and the sodality. One morning I got an email from someone in the HR department saying that people in the office were upset because my team didn't seem to be pulling their weight. "Huh?" I thought. They went on to say the youth ministry team was not in the office all day like other departments were and people were upset about this. Now the funny thing is that I had been tracking my team's hours. They had been putting in around fifty-two to fifty-five hours a week, and that was a normal week without a weekend activity or event. I was also observing that my team had been spending way too much time in the office. I did want them to be in the office, but—at most—only half of

122

the working day. The other half of their time needed to be on school campuses with students, teachers, and administrators or with parents and volunteer leaders.

But see, the modality, which can get caught up in policy and compliance, often forgets the mission of the church as a "sending" agency. Or, sometimes even worse, youth workers feel so much pressure to comply that they become the modality themselves and legitimately forget they're the "sent" ones. (My goodness, get out of the office!)

But with this heavy expectation to grow the youth group, to reach the community, but to also to be in the office all day long, youth workers are at a loss. So then in response and because of all the pressure, we become maintainers—we stop reaching, we turn inward, we comply, and we become nine-to-five worker bees and just simply try to survive. We join the inward-facing modality. Now there's nothing wrong with the modality—we have to have structures, we have to have an HR department; but we cannot forget the sodality part of our job.

Not long ago I was at a youth ministry conference, and one of the speakers was talking about how youth pastors needed to grow up and become professional. He spoke with a sort of arrogance and had a bit of a disrespectful tone and posture, but I did my best to be open to what he was saying. But basically he had two main points: First, that youth workers needed to be in the office all day; and second, that we needed to dress like professionals.

The hilarious thing was that I was sitting next to the very next speaker at the event. He was one of the youth pastors at Saddleback; and he was wearing a ball cap, a Quicksilver t-shirt, and board shorts. He leaned over to me and said, "Well, I guess I better change my clothes really quick before I get up there to speak next."

Now do I think we should dress like fifteen-year-olds when we're meeting with the vestry or the elder board? Probably not—know your audience, right? But, in fact, I only stopped dressing like I was fifteen about five years ago. (Yeah, I know that might have been too long.) So, don't get me wrong, there is some wisdom to what the speaker was saying. I have been a huge proponent of bringing legitimacy to youth ministry as a vocation. It's just as valid and valuable as being (as some might say) a "real" pastor, but we can't forget who our target audience is and what our role and calling is. We aren't the business arm of the church, we're the frontline workers on the edge of culture and we're called the sodality.

Now to help the modality get this vision of what we're about, I started a habit years ago of walking around the office once a week to tell stories—stories of the youth I was working with and reaching. I'd tell anyone who was willing to listen—the receptionist, the maintenance crew, pastors in different departments. And I'd carry the vision of reaching out and coming alongside these teens. If the modality didn't get the vision, I'd carry it for them and to them. I started seeing a difference in how folks in the office viewed what we were doing.

But occasionally even that doesn't work.

THE RADICAL CALLING

I remember sitting at the National Youth Workers Convention (NYWC) in the mid-'90s hearing Mike Yaconneli speak about getting fired for the glory of God. He was talking about the smallness of the church, the mentality that keeps us in our place and causes us to make little cultural difference. He was speaking to a room full of radical youth workers who were longing to reach a troubled generation for Christ, but whose churches wanted them to get more teens in the room and not ask for a raise or larger budget or to use the church's gym for game night—just keep the status quo. I remember listening with longing and feeling inspired by the truth of what he was saying.

Since then I've fought the battles. Yes, I've even been fired, and—to be honest—I'm a bit weary of it all. I've done my part for the past twenty-seven years to reach a generation for the cause of Christ and help carry this vision to churches around the world on behalf of youth workers in this difficult calling. And I'm surprisingly still in the game.

But perspective is always needed. I went for a walk last night with my dad. He told me about a time when he was praying and he sensed God asking him, "Have I ever asked you to trust anyone?"

My dad said he thought for a minute and then told God, "I'm not sure, but I feel like you've wanted me to trust people and to do ministry with people whom I can trust."

God asked again, "Have I really asked you to trust anyone?"

My dad began to think of Bible verses about putting his trust in people, and he couldn't think of a single one.

Then he sensed God say, "Remember, I just asked you to *love* and *serve* every person you come into contact with. I've only asked you to trust *me*. You can trust me."

Here's the truth: *You can trust the One who called you to this amazing and divine calling.*

The crazy thing is that he chose you because he actually thinks you can do it. You can make a difference in that place and in those schools and in the lives of the youth around you. In fact, this is what he's called you to! Remember who you are; you're the sodality.

I love the book of 2 Timothy, and when I read it I like to imagine that I'm young Timothy—overwhelmed, in over his head, and feeling like giving up. This isn't hard for me to imagine at all. His calling was to the Ephesian people who had embraced hedonism in the extreme—talk about a difficult calling. That's some tough terrain. But I imagine being Timothy and one day someone delivers a scroll from my mentor, Paul the Apostle. I imagine slowly unrolling it and then reading these words I'm so desperately longing to hear:

Paul, an apostle of Christ Jesus by the will of God, in keeping with the promise of life that is in Christ Jesus,
To Timothy, my dear son:
Grace, mercy, and peace from God the Father and Christ Jesus our Lord.

[Author's note: I read that and I think:
This is exactly what I need.
I'm desperate for grace, mercy, and peace.]

I thank God, whom I serve, as my ancestors did, with a clear conscience, as night and day I constantly remember you in my prayers. Recalling your tears, I long to see you, so that I may be filled with joy. I am reminded of your sincere faith,
which first lived in your grandmother Lois and in your mother Eunice and,
I am persuaded, now lives in you also. For this reason I remind you to fan into flame
the gift of God, which is in you through the laying on of my hands. For the Spirit God gave us does not make us timid, but gives us power,
love and self-discipline. So do not be ashamed of the testimony about our Lord

or of me his prisoner. Rather, join with me in suffering
for the gospel, by the power of God.
- 2 Timothy 1:1-8 (NIV)

The amazing thing is that these words still resonate with us today, even 2,000 years later. Honestly, I've tried to get out of this calling multiple times, but God won't let me go. You may feel the same in the midst of amazing ministry married with incredible suffering, but for whatever reason God is asking you to fan the flame of that radical calling. Know this: He is not only with you and in you but he actually believes you can do it.

Amen.

*If you ask me what I came to do in this world, I, an
artist, will answer you:
I am here to live out loud.*
– Emile Zola

CHAPTER 9
BEETLES, GTI'S, AND FORGETFULNESS

I sat in an old 1970s Volkswagen Bug about three years ago. Man, it brought back so many awesome memories. It's funny how all old VW Bugs smell the same. My first car was a 1977 silver Beetle with a sunroof that leaked. But I began saving my money when I was thirteen years old. By the time I was fifteen, I had enough to buy it all by myself. Of course, I couldn't drive it for another six months until my sixteenth birthday, as far as my parents knew anyway. But on the day I got my license, I immediately drove over to my friend Rudy's house to pick him up and hit the road. We drove for hours all over the DC area, and boy were we in heaven. There was such freedom and hope and flat-out joy—and we felt legit. (Back then, we were "2 legit 2 quit.")

Man, I loved that car.

But to be honest, after a few years I slowly started to hate that thing. It would break down quite frequently, it was slow, and not only did the sunroof leak but over time when I'd hit a water puddle, water would splash up through the floorboards from below. I started longing for an upgrade to a GTI. In fact, I began to completely forget why I bought that stupid car in the first place.

I first went into youth ministry at the ripe old age of eighteen (almost nineteen). When I began ministry, honestly, I was on cloud nine. Right before I started, I had gone through a season of seeking God and asking the big questions that emerging adults ask, like: "God, what are you calling me to give my life to?" And fortunately I found out early, so all through college I became involved in ministering to young people.

When I started out, it brought me so much life and joy—in fact, the first eight to twelve years of ministry was nonstop awesomeness. Not that there wasn't hard stuff or difficulty or stress. But, those twelve years were mostly a joy-filled season. But then something happened. I'm not even sure what it was. Maybe it was a combination of things.

Here, let me make a list:

- An extremely low paycheck (with no hope for higher pay anytime soon) and really crummy benefits
- Church staff meetings that began to snuff the life out of me
- A tough supervisor who I didn't feel safe with (plus, all he cared about were numbers)
- Not having a voice in shaping language and culture church-wide
- Youth not connecting with the larger church body and getting pushback from the larger church when I would try to implement integration
- The heartbreaking work of watching youth struggling, hurting themselves, falling into addiction, and walking away from faith
- Not feeling known, understood, or respected by staff and church members (I'd hear the old, "So, when are you going to become a real pastor?" thing or, "So, when you're not in the office, what are you doing anyway?" Ugh.)
- Never feeling safe to take time off to recharge
- The constant struggle to get the hires and budget that would allow for the growth we were experiencing

Each of these—or a combination of this stuff to differing degrees—began to take its toll.

Big time.

I started to forget why I even got into youth ministry at all. Like my VW Beetle, the holes in the floorboard and the leaky sunroof were just no longer endearing.

But honestly, you know, I never got tired of sleeping on the floor at camp or on a mission trip. (Thank God for inflatable mattresses.) I never got tired of going to teens' games or recitals or listening to them at coffee shops or dealing with and supporting struggling parents. I never got tired of pursuing youth daily in the midst of the noise and busyness of their lives. I never got tired of their questions and doubts. All of that was fine, even great. But that list of other stuff was leaving me with little joy.

I had serious thoughts about becoming a car salesman or a UPS guy driving around in brown shorts and listening to ESPN radio all day.

A number of years ago, on a Wednesday afternoon, I began setting up for youth group—like every week—and out of nowhere I started having a panic attack. Now, I knew it was a panic attack because I'm a youth worker. I work with young people who have them all the time. But me? Crazy. Now this began to happen from time to time for about two months. Finally, I went and got some counseling. (And, by the way, it helped me significantly.) But I couldn't believe that ministry, which had started out being so wonderful and life-giving, had turned out to bring me such overwhelming stress and hardship.

I began thinking about the environment teens were (and are) living in and why they're having stress and why many are having regular panic attacks. I wanted to know if I was living and thinking similarly to the youth I was trying to help.

Teenagers today:

Feel hopeless. **(So, how is my hope?)**

They're full of fear. **(What am I afraid of?)**

They feel undue and ridiculous pressure. **(What kind of pressure am I feeling?)**

They're believing lies about themselves. **(What lies have I begun to believe?)**

They have forgotten who they really are. **(In the midst of all of this, have I forgotten who I am?)**

They're living daily in an environment (school, friends, family, teachers) where they don't feel safe. **(Am I living in a similar environment?)**

The enemy is trying to steal life from them. **(Have I forgotten that there even is an enemy?)**

They aren't feeding their souls. **(Do I have a daily/weekly/ monthly rhythm that feeds my soul?)**

I needed to reevaluate everything about my life.

I needed to remember some things I had once known, that had fallen by the wayside.

When I sat in that Volkswagen Bug about three years ago, I started to remember how I once thought and lived and how everything felt so free and light. I began to remember the truth about the story I was living in.

I love these verses in *The Message Bible*:

> *Dear, dear Corinthians, I can't tell you how much I long for you to enter this wide-open, spacious life. We didn't fence you in. The smallness you feel comes from within you. Your lives aren't small, but you're living them in a small way. I'm speaking as plainly as I can and with great affection. Open up your lives. Live openly and expansively.*
> **– 2 Corinthians 6:11-13 (MSG)**

And as I sat there in that VW, it all started coming back to me. I longed to live openly and expansively. I wanted to live a wide-open and spacious life. In fact, I knew if something didn't happen soon, I wasn't going to make it.

A few weeks later I spoke at a youth camp, and a teen asked me during a Q and A time how I first got into youth ministry. I started telling the crowd of young people story after story, and we were laughing… and then there were even moments of warm, beautiful emotion. It was like being in that Beetle.

Sometimes we have to remember, because sometimes we forget.

I realized I was allowing people, circumstances, and my own shortcomings and habits to dictate how I was living and feeling and thinking. As I think about it, I have never worked in the perfect church or organization, like ever. No one has. So, how do these lifers make it for thirty or forty or even fifty years of ministry in said organizations and churches? I wondered if I needed a reboot, and I wondered if it really was just me who had the problem.

DIFFICULT CURRENTS

We live near an amazing river just outside of Washington DC.

If you follow it about an hour out of the city, you'll stumble upon an epic place to kayak. One day I headed out with absolute determination to get away, gain perspective, and find where God was in all of the mess.

There's this passage in Galatians 2 where Paul the Apostle gets away and heads out—more than likely—to Arabia, where his hero Elijah had gone a few hundred years earlier. See Paul, like Elijah, just needed perspective, he needed to get away. In fact, Elijah was dejected and massively depressed, verging on suicide; and so he went off to Mount Sinai to meet his God afresh, to learn about the still small voice as well as the earthquake, wind, and fire. There is a necessary pattern for our lives of getting away, unplugging, and actually slowing down long enough to practice what we preach. And we see this discipline throughout the whole narrative of the Scriptures.

So, I got into my Jeep and headed to the river for a day of reflection and, of course, some epic kayaking. But when I arrived, the kayak seemed heavier than normal to carry to the water's edge. I got in and headed downstream and what normally was life-giving was difficult. The paddle didn't feel right and navigating the currents seemed more difficult to me than ever before. I felt uncoordinated, and I just wanted to call it a day, give up, and head back home to the mess of my life. But something kept me going, not to mention my ride was waiting about two more hours downstream. But after about an hour of difficult and heavy paddling, I pulled over to an inlet in the water to take a break, eat my packed lunch, and get my bearings. As I was sitting there eating and watching the water go by, I suddenly felt something. My focus settled in on the sticks and debris and even some garbage floating by.

It's strange how God, seemingly out of nowhere, can reveal things to us and break through all the noise of our lives. I sensed God in that moment say, "Brock, this junk, this stuff in your life that is weighing you down—I'm moving it all away from you, downstream. But you have to let it go. The fear, the stress, the worry—drop it in the water and I'll wash it away. I'll take it far downstream, and I'll deal with it all. Let it go."

I felt like God was commanding me, like he wasn't playing games. He was tired of me believing lies, living a heavy existence. He wanted to take me back to the beginning. He wanted me to live freely and lightly.

I repented right then and there.

As you probably know, to repent means to change your mind and to head in a completely different direction. It's like if you're in Washington DC and you're wanting to go to New York City. You're on this exciting road trip, but suddenly you begin noticing signs for North Carolina. Well, my friend, if you are seeing signs for North Carolina there is definitely something wrong, and you need to make a change. You need to make a choice. You've got to choose as quickly as possible to get off on the next off-ramp, do a U-turn, and start heading north up the 95.

See, I was heading in the wrong direction. In fact, I'm convinced I was heading to a life as a car salesman or a UPS driver. Not that there is anything wrong with those careers, but for me there is. Because I'm called, along with you, to live a different existence and help usher in a movement that I'm convinced will begin with our youth.

I finished my lunch and jumped back into my kayak and everything was completely different. I felt in tune with the river's currents this time and there was an ease to the paddling. I was smiling and hooting and hollering the rest of the way down that river. In fact, what I was really doing was worshipping. I was no longer fenced in, I was free—free to be myself again and full of joy and peace.

LIVING WELL

When I started getting my life back together after that season of extreme stress, I needed to get back to the heart of what life really is about. I also needed to make some hard decisions. In that situation, I even had to quit my job to continue to live out my true calling.

Youth ministry isn't easy. In fact, it's really hard. But I love it, and sometimes I need to be reminded of that. I know why you are pouring out all your time and energy and passion for young people. I get it. You're called. And this calling, it's divine. So, guard it, protect it, and preserve it as best as you can in order to live a beautiful life, to daily make room for your soul—not letting the noise of life or anything else take it from you. Not even the ridiculous expectations from your supervisor or from yourself.

You must live life well and then invite youth into that spacious living. And you must remember. Remember that God's hand is upon you and he is with you. You have been called; and you are favored and anointed; and he has given you a voice this generation needs to hear.

Sit in his amazing peace today. Sit in his presence. Life is good.

for·bear·ance
fôrˈberəns, fərˈberəns/
noun formal
noun: **forbearance**
1. patient self-control; restraint and **tolerance**.
"**forbearance from** taking action"

CHAPTER 10
THE ACTS OF TOLERATION

As I've mentioned, my family and I live about a mile outside of Washington DC in an awesome urban Maryland community called the National Harbor. There is constant activity here with concert events, shopping, and restaurants; and it even has a walking path along the Potomac River and across the Woodrow Wilson Bridge that leads you into Old Town Alexandria.

We love living here. One day we were doing the walk and we stumbled into an area that had a few different plaques with some of the history of Maryland written on them, and that's when I saw it.

The Acts of Toleration was a law passed in 1649 that outlined a policy of punishment and fines for intolerant behavior. The plaque went on to describe a man by the name of George Calvert, a Catholic convert who had a dream. He dreamed of a colony where both Catholics and Protestants could live and prosper together. Before the dream was realized, George passed away; but what didn't die was that dream. This dream lived on in the heart and mind of his son, whose name was Cecil Calvert. Cecil shared his father's commitment to religious toleration, urging both Catholics and Protestants to sail to "Terra Mariae" (as it was then known) to establish the new colony in 1633. So, Catholics and Protestants alike moved there and established a colony that flourished and grew.

When I read this on that family walk, I couldn't get it out of my mind. See, I have a dream as well that has been bubbling inside of me for many years. For as long as I can remember I have seen the infighting of individual churches, and I've grieved at the tearing apart of those churches. I've also seen new denominations developed and the dismissiveness by some regarding other churches' theology. I've been broken over the Catholic and Protestant schism and the lack of honor and mutual respect between the two. For about fifteen years now I have done my best to bring groups together, to preach unity, and to be that person who stands in the middle as a peacemaker.

In fact, I was speaking not long ago at a youth worker event and mentioned in the middle of my session that I believe we needed to re-embrace tolerance. I said "re-embrace" because I wanted the audience to know that there is precedent for churches showing grace and tolerance and even a law passed in the 1600s to ensure it. Now I know the word comes with some heavy baggage, which is why I've been choosing to use it since I wrote *Youth Ministry in a Post-Christian World*. It gets the whole room a bit uncomfortable and then hopefully allows me to reframe and stretch the compartments we as Christians have grown so used to.

After I spoke, a very kind woman came up to me and told me she didn't like the word *tolerance*. She said she loved my talk but that point had thrown her for a loop. I asked why and she said the word *tolerant* in our culture has been applied to every group in the world but Christians. That everyone talks about showing tolerance to everything and everyone, but not toward Christians. Of course, I know this and have experienced it firsthand, but I walked away from that conversation kind of plagued.

I think what really bugged me and is continuing to bug me is that because many Christians believe they aren't being treated fairly or accepted or heard or whatever, they believe they're allowed to respond with intolerance, with anger, with noise. The idea of turning the other cheek doesn't seem to apply to these Christ-followers.

The other thing I've heard from people is that what I'm really talking about is love, and I should move away from the word *tolerance* and just talk about love. I get that; but again, I think it's missing the point.

A couple of years ago I was flying home from a weekend of speaking to youth at a camp. I was exhausted in a wonderful kind of way. There's nothing like speaking into the hearts, minds, and souls of youth and seeing God do amazing things. In fact, I'm addicted to it. But when I got on the plane, all I wanted to do was put my headphones on and take a nap. However, as I took a seat against the window of the plane, two people who were already engrossed in conversation sat right next to me. I couldn't help myself, I had to eavesdrop.

In fact, half of the plane could hear their conversation. They were really funny and really loud. My kind of people. I started to laugh out loud when one of them said she didn't think Christians would even vote for Jesus if he ran for president. Now when I laughed, they both turned to me. I apologized, but they quickly asked me what I did for a living. I smirked and told them hesitantly that I was a pastor. Now they were really intrigued. We started having the most amazing and delightful conversation I have ever had on a plane, and they felt the same way. In fact, when we landed they both thanked me and said it was the most pleasant conversation either of them had ever had with a stranger.

Through our conversation, I found out they both worked for the Democratic party. I told them about my work and my heart for this generation of teens. But here's why I tell you this story: When they found out I spoke around the country to youth, the tone got serious in a beautiful kind of way. One of them looked at me and said, "You are teaching this generation about tolerance, right?" So, I began to paint a picture of this dream I had of mutual respect, honor, listening more than talking, living with a sense of humility and awe—and they shared that dream.

BEING JESUS, NOT JONAH

You know, I have always thought of Jesus as the most tolerant person in history. I find him to just be so very good at it. It makes me wonder if followers of God hate this about him. In fact, it reminds me of the story of Jonah. He had very good reasons to hate the Ninevites. It was the capitol city of Assyria and, as you probably know, the Assyrians were known to be violent, committing mass atrocities that are still talked about to this day. And Jonah thought, like many of us would have, that the world would just be better off without them. But God had a heart for them. He had a dream, a dream to transform them not destroy them. I love the passage where Jonah starts complaining about how tolerant God is in Jonah 4:1-4:

> But to Jonah this seemed very wrong, and he became angry. He prayed to the Lord, "Isn't this what I said, Lord, when I was still at home? That is what I tried to forestall by fleeing to Tarshish. I knew that you are a gracious and compassionate God, slow to anger and abounding in love, a God who relents from sending calamity. Now, Lord, take away my life, for it is better for me to die than to live."
> But the Lord replied, "Is it right for you to be angry?"
> **– Jonah 4:1-4 (NIV)**

I so love the honesty in this story. But I also love the heart of God shown here in the Old Testament that gets fully displayed when he comes to us in the person of Jesus.

And I want to dive a little deeper into this very controversial word *tolerance* for a moment. There are reasons why Christians do not like it. Now, I grew up in the 1980s, and the world

144

today is a very different world than the one I grew up in. As Christians, we're struggling to acclimate to a culture that is no longer sympathetic to our faith.

So, how do we respond?

Do we get louder? *(Maybe if I yell, they will understand the words that are coming out of my mouth.)*

Do we push our weight around and throw a temper tantrum until we get our way?

Maybe we should be full of fear about what is happening right now and create a holy huddle—a Christian bubble, secluded from the world?

Or, do we try to do what James told us to do? He said everyone should be quick to listen, slow to speak, and slow to become angry.

Maybe we should be tolerant of the world and those who are different than us. Let me clarify.

Here's a good definition of tolerance, so you know what I mean by it:

> **Tolerance**: *A fair, objective, and permissive attitude toward those whose opinions, beliefs, practices, racial or ethnic origins, etc., differ from one's own; freedom from bigotry.*[10]

I like that. The word *love* is just too broad and vague concerning the issues today. It doesn't quite do it. We really need this word *tolerance*.

But it's a tough one, especially when we see the great

emergence of post-Christianity.

BACK TO THE BULLY

I remember when I was in middle school, there was another student who was much bigger than the rest of us. He towered above us and he even had full armpits of hair. We were all very impressed with the onset of his puberty, but honestly, we didn't like him very much. He was a bully. I remember being terrorized by him every day. But what's funny is that within a couple of years we all grew past him. In fact, he began to look kind of puny. I remember when he started noticing our growth spurts, it actually caused him to increase his bullying antics— doing his best to keep us intimated. Eventually we all got bigger and he got more pitiful.

Culturally, we've see this happen a lot throughout history. As I explained in chapter three, when those in power begin to lose their authority, their voice, their influence, they can pitch quite a fit. And we know this is happening right now in America. To be honest, I believe this is a good thing for the church. Losing cultural influence is a necessary corrective to arrogant Christian witness with political and cultural dominance.

And it's hard for a bully to lose his or her power. Meanwhile the rest of the kids have learned to get along, to embrace one another's differences. And maybe it isn't fair to call the church a bully, but it has at least been *perceived* this way. Perception carries a lot weight, and normally there's some truth to how we are perceived.

We've already touched on the church's partnership with politics here in the US. In the late 1970s and into the 1980s, the Christian right's partnership with the Republican party gave rise to a very political type of Christianity. This, for a while, gave the religious right power in numbers. But now we see another shift happening and many in the church aren't

146

happy about it. We see Christians fighting for America to "stay Christian" or return to its "Christian roots."

We have the:

> "Ten Commandments at the Capitol" battle
> "Prayer in School" battle
> "Defense of Traditional Marriage" battle
> "Immigration" battle
> "Right to Bear Arms" battle
> "Fake News vs. Real News" battle

It's very interesting to watch and, honestly, a bit disturbing to me. A couple of years ago there was the infamous Starbucks red cup controversy, where Christians were outraged the coffee chain removed typical symbols of the Christmas season—like reindeer, trees, holly, snowmen—from their holiday season cups. And we saw a post-Christian world baffled that Christians would have the audacity to push such an agenda, trying to force a secular company to print traditional symbols of the Christmas season onto a paper cup. (Ugh.)

But the battle isn't just with culture and the church. The church is having all kinds of battles with itself.

I remember sitting in a room of elders with one of my best friends. He asked me to join him because he knew it could be a tough meeting. He couldn't have been more correct. They spoke with overwhelming arrogance, critiquing his speaking, his leadership, his personality—and all of this with an overwhelming air of disrespect toward a guy who had given them his time, energy, love, and gifts for years. I sat there quietly appalled. But my friend did what I had always seen him do. He gave them what he was not receiving from them. He gave them respect and honor and responded with warmth and loving kindness. He was extremely patient. I couldn't believe what I was seeing and hearing. I wanted to stand up and curse them all out or maybe start a fist fight. I wanted to charge the mound like Bryce Harper and punch someone in the face. (I've obviously got some growing to do.) But my friend showed nothing but tolerance and grace. It was startling.

TRUE TOLERANCE

If you are in the lives of youth, which I'm guessing you are, I can tell you responding with tolerance is attractive. Not fear, not hate, not yelling, not those natural responses that are common for those who are losing their influence. Tolerance. What if we became the most grace-filled, loving, and accepting people on the planet? What if the church was the safest place on earth?

My wife, who has just a little bit more emotional intelligence than me, came to me yesterday and said, "Do you think you really should be writing about this, with us launching a new ministry and being at a new church? It seems kind of controversial, and people might get upset." I have thought the same thing, but I'm hoping you're allowing me to reframe the word a bit for you. Hopefully you're journeying with me and you haven't dismissed me. I think what she's saying does have merit. The church may not be the safest place to explore an idea. But I'm hoping we can change that as youth ministers and help prepare this younger generation to be effective in today's ever-changing landscape. Which is the point, isn't it?

I really believe the next ten years for us is critical. I see a movement coming, if we can get a few things right. The fifteen-year-olds in your youth group will be twenty-five in 2027. How will we have prepared them to live in a world that is no longer sympathetic to their faith?

I think the greatest pictures of true tolerance are wise old sages. And really, they don't even have to be old. My father just might

148

be one of the greatest examples of this. I've watched him over the years do a few things and have experienced his *sage*-ness firsthand. This is a man who breaks out a notepad when I am talking and takes notes… of me. (What?)

He does this for others as well. Here's what he does: He sees something in people no one else sees. He's patient with their journeys, allowing them to be whoever they are in that moment. He trusts the Holy Spirit with their journeys. And he's always allowed them to land in a different place than he is—he respects their personal conclusions and is intrigued, with humble curiosity, by how they got there. Then he will even affirm their thinking. That honest and humble posture causes people to truly feel safe. Because they actually are. An authentic and tolerant posture breaks down so many walls.

I was driving with a few guys in Northern California and we passed by a large and very influential church. One of them blurted out, "Man, I hate that place. You know, they really are a cult!"

Honestly, I was shocked by the labeling and the dismissiveness this guy showed. So, I decided to try my sage on. "Really?" I responded. "I haven't heard that. What makes them a cult?"

He quickly responded with, "You know, they are over the top with the Holy Spirit stuff and are setting people up for huge disappointment."

In my mind, I thought, "Wow, being really into the indwelling Spirit of Jesus and occasionally disappointing people, makes you a cult, hmm?" (See Romans 8:9.)

I bring this up because the church doesn't even show tolerance toward one another, let alone a world that is dying to experience grace and love from it. We really should read the beginning of Philippians 2. It might help us a bit. After all, Paul tells us in Titus that grace teaches us to say no to ourselves (Titus 2:12). Grace is what ignites change in people, not judgment, not intolerance.

This is one of the topics that kills me. I speak in all kinds of churches and denominations all over the country, and I see Jesus in all of them, everywhere I go. I hate the church's intolerance towards the church. No wonder the world doesn't trust us.

Let me just clarify what I'm saying for a second:

> Tolerance does not mean we have to change our values.
> Tolerance does not mean we don't think sin is sin.
> Tolerance doesn't mean we are no longer allowed to have our own opinions.
> Tolerance gives us patience for people's journeys.
> Tolerance has ears, not just a mouth.
> Tolerance is a posture that softens our hearts and keeps fear from filling them.
> Tolerance remembers that we're in the business of loving the "other," not manipulating their conversions.
> Tolerance is married to grace, and grace is something we all need.
> Tolerance allows for alternate views, recognizing that we don't know it all.
> Tolerance is the opposite of control.

If we actually acted out tolerance, in the way I'm defining it, it would look a lot like love. ("Love is patient, love is kind. It does not envy, it does not boast, it is not proud" [1 Corinthians 11:4, NIV].) I know I said love doesn't quite encompass it, but stay with me. See, with the re-embracing of tolerance, we are

150

using language the world is using. Tolerance is a value in our world today, and I just think we should out-tolerance the world.

So, what does this mean for youth today? Well, teenagers— and the world in general—see how everyone in society shows tolerance except the church. To me, this is unacceptable and really does cause our youth to fake it—not being honest with where they're at, with what they're struggling with. They're afraid they will be met with *in*tolerance in their churches.

The church basically needs more sages. Men and women who will journey with people, allowing God to be the judge and doing their best to love—to be teens' deep-spirited friends. Does this mean we don't help teens and we don't speak truth into their lives? No, we must. We know that the gospel is for the flourishing of all things and all people. The gospel is good news for all of creation. We want to humbly demonstrate what flourishing looks like, living really well ourselves and creating an atmosphere in which youth feel safe. When they know we love them, no matter what, then we can humbly speak loving truth. Not from the stage, telling the whole room that those who are struggling with their sexuality (which could be a decent percentage of the room these days) are not only sinning, but they're in danger of hell. (Ugh.) No, we are careful, thoughtful with how we communicate. We create an environment where youth can experience the warmth of God. That's tolerance.

Tolerance is personal, not up front on the stage venting.

Last story: A teen in our youth group once told her small group she had kissed another girl and was feeling really guilty about it. She genuinely felt she was getting into a myriad of behaviors that were not healthy and this was just a part of that. At this point another teen spoke up and said this type of behavior was really wrong—that she was sinning. The awful result was that the girl who confessed became aggressive and defensive. Lack of tolerance changed a moment of confession into a moment of alienation. It caused her to stop coming to our youth group for a long time. Warmth/grace/love/tolerance does the opposite. It invites people in to stay.

The dream of the Calvert boys from Maryland is bidding us to join in the movement.

I'm ready.

*What can I say about Milton Berle that he hasn't
already said himself?*
– George Burns

CHAPTER 11
WHY THE FUTURE IS DESPERATE
FOR THE HUMBLE

I used to be on the Youth Specialties National Speaking team. Youth Specialties (YS) ran a youth worker training event called The Core in over a hundred cities around the US and Canada, as well as in every Spanish-speaking nation in the world. It was amazing, and I felt so honored to be on that team. Now, if you're new to youth ministry—or if you're reading this book but you're not an actual youth worker—you may not know this, but the work of youth ministry is highly competitive. There's a lot of "So, how many kids are in your youth group?" stuff, and there are jealousies and other bits of nonsense. If I ever started to get a big head from being on the YS speaking team, I'd soon be brought down to earth. Once in a while, a youth worker would come to the event, hear me speak, and walk up to me afterwards and say something like, "So, how in the world did *you* ever get on *this* speaking team?" I'd smirk and tell them to get lost and we'd move on. But seriously, I remember having similar thoughts when I wasn't on the team.

Then when I would speak someone would occasionally ask me if I knew how he or she might be able to get onto the speaking team, and I'd be super positive and tell them to email Tic Long. I'd say that he'd love to hear from them, and of course he absolutely hated when I'd do that, which is why I did it.

But the whole thing made me super uncomfortable. The system was almost set up where every youth worker wanted to be famous—be an author or speaker or have a famous blog. It really got to be a bit nauseating. Instead of seeking justice, loving mercy, and walking humbly with our God, we were seeking fame, loving attention, and walking arrogantly with our own egos.

Our church's youth ministry team had the privilege of attending the Holy Trinity Brompton Church Leadership Conference in London this past year. This is my absolute favorite conference by far, and I try to get out there each year for it. Every time I'm there I'm amazed at how diverse the conference is. They bring in leaders from all over the world—leaders who do not look like them, do not have the same economic standing as them, do not speak the same language as them. But there are two things most of them have in common: First, they're all in leadership positions somewhere; and second, they're driven by a belief that motivates them.

One of the things that makes this conference unique is that they invite speakers from every walk of life. Not everyone there is a Christian, but they are all interested in and rooting for one another. Because that's what leaders do—they contribute to the lives of others, they're always investing in the people placed in front of them. Leaders empower other people to do great things and to discover the answer to this question: *Why?* Why do they do what they do? And if they cannot answer that question, good leaders help those around them answer it. Otherwise they will be unable and even deficient to lead themselves. But if they can answer the question, they're empowered and they know what their personal value is.

As followers of Christ and people called to usher the kingdom of God into the everyday lives of those around us, my great hope is that we have all landed on why we do what we do. The issue that grieves my heart about today's church leadership is that many of us are living under the delusion that fame follows reach. We look to the anomalies and hold them up as the standard-bearers of our ministry and our aspirations, instead of recognizing that leadership has almost nothing to do with being famous, well-known, having a popular podcast or blog, or having thousands attend your church.

I know, you might be thinking it's easy for me to say, because here you are reading a book I wrote and possibly on occasion you might peruse my blog or you might have heard me speak at a conference or a retreat. So, am I telling you I'm an anomaly?

Well, the answer to that would be yes. Yes, I'm an anomaly. I have had the distinct pleasure of gaining a platform quite by accident or perhaps providence. I'm not really sure which. But here's the thing, most of us are just in the right place at the right time, and we happen to know the right people who helped us out. But none of it is the point or the purpose of what God's called us to. I'm not even sure if I like the position I'm in.

But back in 2004, I was attending the NYWC; and Tic Long, the president of events at YS, came up to me and started a conversation. Eventually he threw this out, "So, what do you think about speaking here at the conference next year? And I'd love for you to apply for a position on our team here at YS." Now let me pause here for a second. At the time, working for YS was—in the world of youth work—like working at Pixar or Disney or maybe like being an executive at Apple. They were the giant in the industry and the competition was barely competition. So, I nearly freaked—like literally almost started jumping up and down when Tic asked me this.

Well, I couldn't sleep that night, and so I got up really early and went across the street from our hotel to a little café. It was about five o'clock in the morning, and I was writing in my journal. This is what I wrote: "Lord, if you really want me to do this, I want you to have Tic walk up to me again and ask me to apply." As soon as I finished writing that line in my journal, Tic walked into the café, sat down at my table, and said, "Have you given any more thought to applying for the gig? I think you'd be great." (I nearly lost it!)

So, when people asked me, "How did someone like *you* get on the speaking team?" I simply say, "It's totally God's fault, and I'm very sorry." (Ha.) But I think that longing for the stage and the platform is missing the point in a big way.

THE WHY

Recently a friend of mine, Caleb, was ordained in the Anglican church. At his ordination, our pastor placed a green sash or vestment around his neck. As he was putting it on him he explained the meaning of it. He said it was green because he was continually going to grow and he'd always be learning. But then he also explained that the reason priests and clergy wear vestments is to remind them they are called to be the servants of the people—that the vestment actually is designed like the towel Jesus used to wash his disciples' feet. Caleb was ordained to service, always to give his best for the betterment of others.

And, you know, this calling is not an easy one. I thank God for secure leaders who aren't afraid to have a unique thought expressed in a unique way and to lift up someone who is just working really hard at what he or she does. It takes guts to lift others up and not take the credit. It takes guts to serve and take the lesser role or to empower others to lead. It takes guts to bring the focus off of yourself and onto someone who could easily someday replace you—that's true leadership. These are people who know why they do what they do, and that is where their value lies—not in the applause or the accolades or the fame. All that fades away; it's nothing but rubble. This is what the future of youth ministry and, I believe, church ministry leadership must look like going forward.

I've been, like so many, wholly inspired by the popular

researcher Simon Sinek. (Yeah, he's kind of all over the place right now.) And as I listened to him speak at the Holy Trinity Brompton Leadership Conference, I was moved by the urgency with which he addressed us as leaders.

Because we've all labeled the upcoming generation. We've listed the things we hate about them—making videos, snarky jokes—and basically washed our hands of them. But as a youth worker, someone in the trenches, I cannot wash my hands or pass them off. If I'm going to do this for the rest of my life—and I plan to—I need to learn how to lead them; so, Simon's work (and the work of others like him) is important for us. But we have to let go of the celebrity mentality and trust God as we learn why we are doing what we are doing and become courageous in that.

One of Simon's points was illustrated with a story about the competitiveness that exists between Apple and Microsoft.

He was booked about a year ago to speak at both Microsoft and Apple. When he went to the Microsoft event he noticed that all they spoke about was how they were going to beat Apple. They spoke about it obsessively; it was their mission. At the end of the Microsoft conference, they gave him one of their new products. Simon said it was the most amazing thing he'd ever seen, far better than Apple's similar product.

But after that, he immediately went to speak at an Apple event. He noticed that Apple never once spoke about Microsoft and out-doing them. Instead they obsessively spoke about how they could better serve teachers, businesses, and companies with their products and support.

After the Apple event, Simon pulled out the Microsoft product and kind of teased an Apple executive saying, "Have you seen this thing? It's way better than your product."

The Apple executive just shrugged his shoulder and smiled. Simon discovered very quickly that the man was not threatened by a better Microsoft product at all, instead he was confident in the higher purpose Apple espouses, which is:

> "Apple is committed to bringing the best personal computing experience to students, educators, creative professionals, and consumers around the world through its innovative hardware, software, and Internet offerings."

Apple is more concerned about making life better for human beings. They know why they do what they do, and they're confident in it—as opposed to trying to win some competition with another company. It's this long-term consistency, which requires commitment and discipline, that wins the hearts and minds of people. They know there's fluctuation and timing with products and sometimes other companies might have better items and sometimes they might not. But the point is the *why*.

A SELFLESS LIFE

Millennial's have been called the "selfie-generation"—a narcissistic, self-consumed lot. But let's be honest, every generation has been like this. We're all a bunch of selfish jerks, aren't we? The earth doesn't revolve around the sun. It revolves around you and me and has been doing so for decades. Any time someone gets a raise or gets a promotion or a book deal, we think, "Why not me?"

But somehow God has chosen us and is capable of transforming this tendency. See, God—rich in mercy—has lifted our heads. He's made us aware of himself and aware of others and, evidently, he actually thinks we can do it. That we can represent him and serve others, loving and believing in them.

For quite a few years, Philippians 2 has become such a theme for me. The first few verses are all about getting along, being deep-spirited friends, and putting others and their needs ahead of our own. Then it goes into how Jesus actually set the tone, the tempo, and paved a way for a selfless life. Check it out in *The Message*:

> *Think of yourselves the way Christ Jesus thought*
> *of himself. He had equal status with God but didn't*
> *think so much of himself that he had to cling to the*
> *advantages of that status no matter what. Not at all.*
> *When the time came, he set aside the privileges of*
> *deity and took on the status of a slave, became human!*
> *Having become human, he stayed human. It was an*
> *incredibly humbling process. He didn't claim special*
> *privileges. Instead, he lived a selfless, obedient life*
> *and then died a selfless, obedient death—and the*
> *worst kind of death at that—a crucifixion.*
> *Because of that obedience, God lifted him high and*
> *honored him far beyond anyone or anything, ever, so*
> *that all created beings in heaven and on earth—even*
> *those long ago dead and buried—will bow in worship*
> *before this Jesus Christ, and call out in praise that he*
> *is the Master of all, to the glorious honor*
> *of God the Father.*
> **– Philippians 2:5-11 (MSG)**

My wife and I had dinner not long ago with another couple who were also in youth ministry at a church here in the DC area. I have to tell you, it was exhausting. Everything felt like a contest. Kelsey and I got into the car afterward and just sank into our seats in utter exhaustion. It's so tiring to live like that and have such shallow, ridiculous conversations. No matter how we tried to steer the conversation, it was puffy and prideful and competitive. I wanted to yell, "Stop it! Just stop it!"

But here's the reality: *You cannot take your youth anywhere you are not.*

The world is desperate for humble, selfless servant-Christians; but it won't ever happen if their leaders aren't there themselves. God is calling us to raise up a generation who will be a part of bringing hundreds of thousands, and maybe more, to Jesus. It will take humility to do it. Humility is so attractive. Service always wins, and people often need to experience good news before they can receive the good news.

About twenty years ago, I heard a speaker talk all about servant leadership. It had such an amazing and profound impact on me that it set in motion some patterns, thoughts, and habits in my life. I remember he ended by reading this amazing work by G. D. Watson. I'd love to end this chapter with this word. I read it regularly, and I hope you will join me.

THE HIGH CALLING
ATTRIBUTED TO: G. D. WATSON

If God is calling you to be truly like Jesus, he will draw you into a life of crucifixion and humility, and put on you demands of obedience that sometimes will not allow you to follow other Christians. In many ways, he will seem to let other good people do things he will not let you do.

Other Christians, and even ministers, who seem very religious and useful, may push themselves, pull strings, and work schemes to carry out their plans; but you cannot do these things. And if you attempt them, you will meet with such failure and rebuke from the Lord as to make you sorely penitent.

Others can brag about themselves, about their work, about their success, about their writings; but the Holy Spirit will not allow you to do any such thing. And if you begin bragging, he will lead you into some deep mortification that will make you despise yourself and all your good works.

Others will be allowed to succeed in making great sums of money, or having a legacy left to them, or in having luxuries. But God may only supply you daily, because he wants you to have something far better than gold—a helpless dependence on him—that he may have the privilege of providing your needs daily out of the unseen treasury.

The Lord may let others be honored and keep you hidden away in obscurity; because he wants to produce some choice, fragrant fruit for his coming glory, which can only be produced in the shade.

God will let others be great, but keep you small. He will let others do a work for him and get the credit for it, but he will make you work and toil without knowing how much you are doing. And then to make your work still more precious, he will let others get the credit for the work which you have done; and this will make your reward ten times greater when Jesus comes.

The Holy Spirit will put such a strict watch on you, with jealous love, and rebuke you for little words and feelings or for wasted time, which other Christians never seem distressed over.

So, make up your mind that God is an infinite Sovereign who has a right to do as he pleases with his own and needs not explain to you a thousand things, which may puzzle your reason in his dealings with you.

God will take you at your word. And if you absolutely sell yourself to be his slave, he will wrap you up in a jealous love and let other people say and do many things you cannot do or say.

Settle it forever that you are to deal directly with the Holy Spirit and that he is to have the privilege of tying your tongue or chaining your hand or closing your eyes in ways that others are not disciplined.

Now, when you are so possessed with the living God that you are, in your secret heart, pleased and delighted over this peculiar, personal, private, jealous guardianship and management of the Holy Spirit over your life, you will have found the vestibule of heaven.

– G. D. Watson

A river is easier to channel than to stop.
– Brandon Sanderson
Shadows of Self

CHAPTER 12
MOMENTUM

Youth Sunday is always a highlight for me after camp. The way youth are able to affirm through testimony the impact of a time away is so vital to their spiritual lives and often to the lives of the whole church family. A few years ago, we returned from our youth mission trip on a Friday, and the teens were leading the main services at our church all that weekend. I remember standing on stage with a few of our young people, fresh from an amazing week together. It was just one of those weekend services that so inspires.

The entire church family encountered Jesus that morning as Billy, standing directly next to me, said, "I grew up atheist, but after this week, I'm a follower of Jesus. God really revealed himself to me."

Next to him was Sammy, who with a soft and broken voice whispered, "After my dad died, I gave up on God and went through a really dark period of self-injury and extreme depression. But this week I sensed God's warm presence inviting me back to himself. I think I'm ready to trust him again."

Next to Sammy was a middle schooler named Brian. His words rang true with all of us when he said, "I feel like an adventure is beginning."

What a morning!

But what we were supposed to do in the weeks that followed is the great youth ministry question. How do we continue the momentum after something like that? How do we keep faith alive? How do we keep the passion? How might this experience lead us into a movement? These are some of the questions we all face.

Call it a camp high, a God-moment, or whatever—I have to tell you, I'm just sick of it all. I long for true transformation for all our youth, our youth leaders, and myself. I long for the reality of those trips—where teens discover who they really are—to bleed into our daily grind back home.

 In a couple of months, we're taking our DC youth group away for the four-day weekend. On the last night, I'm going to say something like, "All weekend we've been up here experiencing true reality, where the divisions and barriers between us have dissipated. Where we have been sharing our hearts together, praying for each other, worshipping God without fear of judgment, opening the Scriptures together, and we've slowed down long enough so that we have actually become aware of God's overwhelming presence. *This* has been the real world, *this* has been true reality—what we're getting ready to go back to is the illusion."

But I know what will happen: We will all get into the buses and head back home; and the cell phones will come out; and the teens will get off the bus; and they'll hit the ground running right back to the noise of their lives.

Unless…

Unless something happens.

———————

We're in the middle of moving to a new house, which is truly quite a blessing, but in true Morgan style we had to paint before we moved in. Eleven hours of priming and painting—plus packing and lugging boxes—for two days now. Boy am I

168

fried. All that and now we're going to take our student leaders away for a weekend retreat. Talk about needing momentum.

And many of us have felt our momentum draining rapidly like that, like brakes screeching, and—as hard as we try—can't seem to drum up the energy to move forward. Or maybe you are ready to roll, but not everyone in your life is on board. If you know where you're headed, uninterrupted momentum is a precious commodity. How might we capitalize on getting away with our teens and opening their hearts to what a spiritual life actually looks like back home? We have to address how we can go back home and continue the things that began on our retreat.

Here's a word of caution: This might end up causing us to rethink some things, and that could be difficult. We may need to come back and make some vital ministry changes. (On the other hand, this could be fun!)

In my ministry and in the ministry of other youth workers across the country, I have seen patterns that steal from momentum. All of these patterns are born out of a lack of intentional planning on our parts. Maybe we're just too tired, worn out from the daily grind of giving our lives away, or just stuck in what we've always done. Maybe we just never really thought about it. I mean honestly, youth Sunday is a win—I've done my job, the entire church family has acknowledged my win, and now it's time to plan next year's calendar. Because that's what it's really about right? Dates on calendars, programs, and showing off once a year to make sure your job is secure?

Believe me, I've been there, I'm still there. These are hard patterns to let go of, because they ensure "success." (Whatever that means.) But it's time to identify these patterns, so we can create a movement and grab ahold of the momentum that started at camp or on our retreat.

MOMENTUM STEALER #1:
SHALLOW YOUTH GROUP

What has deeply grieved me this past election season has been the appeal to the most basic human desires. The lowest common denominator in society has been held up as the standard. We are no longer about others; we are no longer about the bigger picture. Instead we holler about our own personal rights. Sometimes our youth groups reflect this same cultural disposition.

It shows up in a couple of ways. The first being fear of the few. Now what I mean by this is the reactionary response we have when a few teens don't like something we're doing. I understand this, because I don't like the feeling in my stomach when people don't approve of something I've done or said. The problem here is that we have prayed, planned, and agonized over the content of our programs. (Hopefully.) But we give ear to a couple of negative teens, parents, and leaders. And their words get blown up in our minds. A couple of young people begin to represent, in our minds, all of the youth in our ministry. We become oversensitive to the couple and forget that we're not trying to appeal to the lowest common denominator. In other words, it's not our job to make everyone happy. If that's in the job description, then I have failed miserably and I don't want any part of it anyhow.

I find it interesting when one of my staff comes up to me concerned and tells me a group of teens were unhappy about something that was said or done one night at youth group. Inevitably I have to ask them, "Exactly how many teens are you talking about?"

It's not that I don't care, I do. I'd love nothing more than to have a chat with disgruntled youth to find out the root of their unhappiness. (Actually, not really.) But to give their words more weight than they deserve is foolishness. Usually the scenario runs that it was one, maybe two, teens and their concerns have more to do with their own personal angst than anything else.

I have also experienced this same thinking when it comes to policy. Now I am all for safety of the youth, but when we take an anomaly and turn it into a reason to implement stricter standards or new policies we sometimes end up squashing ministry opportunities. I recently consulted with a local youth pastor friend who is dealing with this very problem. A troubled youth insinuated one of his volunteers had been rough with him physically. Fortunately, in this case there was a second adult volunteer who vouched for the innocence of the accused volunteer, but this did not stop the policymakers from proposing the youth group no longer have overnight events... at all. My friend was deeply grieved because so much of ministry happens when we get away for a period of time with teens. This always involves spending the night somewhere, so you can see the dilemma. When we give in to the anomaly, the lowest common denominator, the exception to the rule, we might be doing a massive disservice to the whole.

How did these examples lead to a shallow youth group?

Well, forgetting the good of the whole can be horribly stifling to the impact of the ministry. Youth ministry is messy, my friends. It's bad enough when policymakers tie our hands. But it's super bad when we tie our own hands out of fear. It's so important that we talk about and do the things that are for the greater good of our youth. Yes, we must consider criticism. Yes, we must take safety precautions. But we must be wise and intentional about how we do ministry for the whole, not reactionary. When we come home from camp or a mission trip, it's vital that our group goes to a deeper place spiritually. That we bring that back to the rest of the group and the programming reflects what has happened—in fact, it should never be the same. We are changed and our programs should reflect this, despite the naysayers.

It's important that we never just move on, that we continue to acknowledge the work of God in our lives as a group. And that requires that we teach, that we hold up examples, and that we constantly remind ourselves and our teens that we were made for so much more. Allowing the naysayers, the complainers, and the exceptions to the rules to dictate our ministry choices has to stop.

MOMENTUM STEALER #2:
NO MINISTRY TIME

Lately I've been seeing a couple of extremes in youth ministry. The programming either looks like a classroom setting or a game show. Rarely is there an in-between and almost never is there space made for God's Spirit to minister to youth. Ironically, we do make that space at camp, because for some reason we think the Holy Spirit only moves within our youth somewhere else. Sadly, I think many of us are afraid to acknowledge God's Spirit working in our teens when we come home to the "real world." There's pressure for sure. There are many of us who deal with parents who are adamant that their child learn systematic theology but aren't concerned with them having an understanding of or experience with God's Spirit. There is fear of the unexplainable, the untamable, the *not* understandable Spirit of God; and many of us just don't like it.

But we've heard the desperate cries of teens at a camp or retreat. They long for a miracle for themselves, for their friends. And they're longing for bold prayers to be prayed over them to a God who actually does stuff in the world today. Regardless of your theology of the Holy Spirit, he is the third person of the Trinity. I wonder if we daily blaspheme God's Spirit by not simply acknowledging he even exists. If we do not make room for our teens to receive the good things God

172

has for them, to have bold prayers prayed and answered, I think we've missed it.

I started at my current church about a year ago, and one of the first things I observed was that we did announcements longer than we prayed.

What in the world are we doing?

THE BEGINNING OF MOMENTUM

So, how do we address these hindrances to our momentum?

We all have a longing to see each of our teens grow and become everything God has for them in the time we have them in our ministries. We also long to see our youth groups become counter-cultural communities, places of transcendence where teens can become a part of a movement—something that is greater than themselves and that is making a difference in our communities and, as a result, the world.

I must confess my least favorite part of youth ministry is coming home after a mission trip. Teens on these getaways have finally begun to live the way of Jesus. They actually have embraced a Spirit-filled life. But then we go back to the busyness and noise of our lives, and over the years I've wondered: *How do we take what we experienced on this trip and continue it back home?* I think we've all thought this.

A few weeks ago, I was speaking to a pretty large youth group. There were a few hundred in the room, and the atmosphere (as you can imagine) was electric with anticipation. There's nothing like a room full of teenagers—absolutely nothing like it.

Before I spoke there was a very entertaining program: hilarious welcome by the interns, a large group game, engaging and fun

173

announcement video, dynamic worship… You know, the basic youth group stuff typical of today. The crazy thing was, the youth pastor asked me to come and talk about how the faith was actually a movement.

See, she had noticed this large group had grown stale, they were stuck. She felt like what they were doing should have been more effective. She said, "We entertain, we give great information, we provide a space to hear the gospel and encounter God's presence, and we build friendships and community." The reality though was that she believed it wasn't actually leading to much of anything. Her fear was that none of it was leading to true transformation or creating youth-group-wide momentum. She and her team were longing for more.

What I found was this: Her teens were also longing for more. What she was feeling was right on the money. The teens were also tired of sitting in the room and just talking about the faith. They were tired of having isolated experiences with God (for the most part, just on trips); they wanted more. They knew, in their minds and because they were told, that God was on the move; and they wanted the God of the Bible to be a part of their lives. They wanted to see God do something, anything. They didn't just want stories about the gloried past, they wanted stories of the here and now. They longed for a vibrant intellectual and spiritual existence rooted deeply in a community of people who were actively participating in what God was doing—*now*.

The youth workers of this community and the youth themselves all wanted the same thing. I actually think it's the cry of all humanity. We are all longing for what was lost in the beginning.

What this group ended up doing was just one thing. I

174

challenged them to start a movement by praying. And they're actually doing it. They became a praying community, and it's literally changing everything. Not just for their youth group but for the community at large.

I think that must be the beginning of momentum: prayer. Desperate pleas for God to bring peace to troubled minds, joy to the heavy hearted, and calling to the purposeless. Prayer leads us back to God's heart—and not just prayer by the leadership. The youth *must* be a part of it.

What if youth ministries became vibrant prayerful communities that sought to create sanctuary and mission? I believe youth are longing for both.

So, that's the call: Pray. I know it seems simple, maybe a bit underwhelming. But what if we actually did it? I wonder.

I've asked a previous student of my youth group, who is now in college, to close this chapter out:

STEWARDING MOMENTUM
BY: TROONE MARCHAK

Momentum. God gave me this word a few weeks ago. I started thinking about how I have experienced momentum and how I see God use it in ministry today. God really spoke to me about how momentum is from him, and how we can't waste it. When God generates momentum for his kingdom in our hearts, it's an invitation for a movement to begin.

I think the momentum that is stirred among youth when they are at camp comes from their eyes being fixed on God. When young people are at camp, on a retreat, or on a mission trip, they are (for the most part) away from the endless distractions of our world.

When they are at camp, they're actually able to rest their gaze on Jesus and spend some uninterrupted time exploring that relationship.

Newton's first law of motion states that an object in a state of uniform motion tends to remain in a state of motion unless an external force is applied to it. I'm not a physicist, but I believe it works the same for our human hearts.

When a teenager goes to camp and his or her heart is "set in motion" by the Holy Spirit, it will continue "in motion." Therefore, a product of our encounters with God is momentum. When our youth have the opportunity to explore and grow in their faith, momentum cannot help but be cultivated. That is the gospel. It's exciting and adventurous—it's a calling. When our eyes are fixed on God and when youth encounter him, they cannot help but be moved to a place of action. Momentum.

Conversely, the fear of failure can often be the "external force" applied to momentum that stops the state of motion. I think what discourages youth from exercising their momentum to step out and do something is the fear of failure. Fear of failure holds us all back. It's what holds me back. As a leader, there have been countless times I have let myself shrink into my fear and not speak out a new idea or share a word God has put on my heart. I find myself justifying my fear by telling myself "you're too young" or "people will think that's a useless idea" or "you don't know enough to make that happen."

For youth leaders and our youth alike, we can conquer this fear of failure by remembering God absolutely loves using his children to transform this world to look more like his kingdom.

The book of Philippians says:

> *Be energetic in your life of salvation, reverent and sensitive before God. That energy is God's energy, an energy deep within you, God himself willing and working at what will give him the most pleasure.*
> **– Philippians 2:12-13 (MSG)**

That word is so significant because the knowledge that our all-powerful Creator God actually works through us for his purposes tells us that failure is actually impossible if we are pursuing his will. Though we have human limitations, our God never fails, because we achieve not in our own strength but by the power of the Holy Spirit within us.

I love what Brock said in this chapter about the power of prayer and the importance of encouraging youth to pray. Prayer sources momentum for young people and provides direction. Rather than feeling overwhelmed by the brokenness of our world, a teenager in prayer may feel called to minister directly to the people in their local homeless shelter or start a campaign to help meet basic needs of other teenagers around the world. When teens know their momentum is backed by their all-powerful and never-failing God, the fear of failure becomes smaller and smaller and the vision of God's kingdom becomes closer and clearer.

– Troone Marchak

*Evangelism is the cure to
the disease of church boredom.*
– Todd P. McCollum

CHAPTER 13
BRINGING GOOD NEWS BACK TO EVANGELISM

I remember the first time I begged young people not to go forward to accept Jesus. (I know that seems a bit disturbing, but hang in there for just a moment.) I remember sitting there with my youth listening to the speaker give what I thought was a beautiful and clear gospel presentation. He then invited forward those who wanted to open their lives up to Jesus.

Now, none of my youth went down to the front, because they were already Christians. I could only get my student leaders to come to an event like this, and they just came to hear Switchfoot before the speaker. Everything was going great, teens were coming forward, the worship band was playing, and adults were down in front to pray with the youth who came forward.

But then it happened, and in an instant everything changed. Out of nowhere the speaker said, "If you have never confessed Jesus publicly, in front of a crowd of people, then you're in danger of eternal torture in hell."

All the youth who were there from our church immediately turned to me. They looked scared out of their minds and asked, "Brock, should we go down front?"

I said, "No. You love Jesus."

But, of course, they all went down front anyway, just in case I was wrong.

Then recently I took my daughter to a Nationals game here in Washington DC, and on our way into the stadium, a gentleman on a very loud speaker system was telling everyone there that we were all going to hell. I don't know, but this didn't seem like very good news to me. Especially because of what happened next. As we passed by him, he looked directly at me. I looked back at him and asked, "Are you talking to me?"

He looked me directly in the eyes and said over his PA system for all to hear, "Yes, you sir. I'm talking to you."

Now, maybe these two examples are just some of the many reasons why more than a few of us throw up a little bit in our mouths when we think of evangelism.

But *the* good news, I think, should be *good* news.

———

In 2009, the Dallas Cowboys were playing the Philadelphia Eagles. Now, I wasn't able to watch it because I was in England, and because of the time difference the game was on while I was asleep. But it was a very important game, and I was anxious about the score. So, I woke up early and went down to the lobby to find a paper. Of course, there were no American football scores in the paper, so I walked over to the front desk and asked the gentleman if he could look it up on his computer. So, there in the lobby, with quite a few other people standing around, I found out the Cowboys did indeed win the game. But I soon discovered that what was good news to me—and for millions of other Cowboy fans—meant nothing to anyone in England. I might as well have gone to Montana and announced on the streets that China had beaten Germany in table tennis. All I would get would be a shrug of the shoulders and a big yawn: "So what?"

Then I ran into someone who liked the Eagles, and what was good news to me was terrible news to him.

See, the good news about Jesus isn't supposed to be like that,

182

though that's the impression people often get. And I think that may be because evangelism doesn't seem like good news, or it may be because it's viewed as some kind of bait and switch or fear tactic or possibly even poaching. Or maybe it's viewed as some political right agenda and not humble interaction or conversation or what is ultimately supposed to be good news about how Love is bringing freedom and wholeness and renewal to all of creation.

So, I want to suggest that we need to get back to the heart of the good news.

Now we could talk all day about the problems and the theological implications of stupid people, but I'd rather just offer some humble thoughts for how we might bring good news back to the good news.

So, how do we bring good news back to evangelism?

1. WE MUST BE AWARE THAT WE ARE NOW LIVING IN A DIFFERENT WORLD.

Not long ago a teen and I met for coffee. He was new to our group, not from a Christian family, but really liking what he was experiencing at our youth group. He wanted to meet with me because he had some questions. Now going in, it was necessary for me to understand some things. First, that he hadn't grown up in the same world I grew up in. Not only was his family different than mine but the culture and world he's growing up in is different, it's a pluralistic one. The dominant voice is no longer coming from a Judeo-Christian perspective. So, I had to be aware that today's world is shaping his thinking, and it's no longer a world that is sympathetic to what this teen had been hearing at our youth group. We are living in the midst of an emerging post-Christian country.

If you still aren't sure about that, from 2007 to 2014 our nation grew by fifteen million people, but Christianity declined by five million people, according to a recent Pew report.[11] Not only is there decline, but we're living in a world where the term "Christian" comes with some pretty heavy baggage. In some circles, it's almost like the word *Nazi*. And much of this is for good reason. Especially if you read Facebook posts by some Christians—it can get pretty ugly.

So, what if we lived with an awareness that we are sitting in a room, we're sitting in a church, with people and with teens who don't believe everything that comes out of our mouths?

No Matter How Loud We Get.

This is a new world. Living with this awareness is so vital as we live and interact in today's world.

2. EVANGELISM TODAY MUST BE MORE ABOUT THE RIGHT QUESTIONS THAN ANSWERS.

So, there we are in Starbucks and he says, "Brock, I just am so unsure about what I'm getting into. The things I've been raised with, what I see Christians saying and how I see them saying it—it all just seems so hateful and judgmental and ignorant."

So, of course, I used my seminary training and asked him, "If you were to die today and you were standing before God and God asked you, 'Why should I let you into my heaven?' what would you say?"

No. No, I didn't Evangelism Explosion the guy. What I needed to do was ask questions *without* a hidden agenda. I needed to shut up and just listen.

I needed to ask questions that didn't come from a place of judgment.

See, the reality is that we have lost our right to be heard. Today's evangelism is about living out James's words:

> *Everyone should be quick to listen, slow to speak and*
> *slow to become angry."*
> **– James 1:19 (NIV)**

This is why I am a big fan of the organization Alpha. That's why I can't help but bring it up again here. It never ceases to amaze me that in the midst of the darkness of Europe was this little movement, gaining steam one meeting at a time. It was designed to just ask questions and guide people into faith. By the time I discovered Alpha, it had already helped thousands upon thousands of young people (and adults) come to Christ in England alone.

A movement was beginning, and it all began with the beautiful big questions of life.

3. EVANGELISM MUST BE A CALL INTO KINGDOM MISSION.

We somehow forgot what evangelism is meant to do. We've turned the gospel into an escape plan out of this world, but that isn't the gospel at all. It's a calling to join a movement of being salt and light and of representing another world, a better world. We have to get away from the narrow view of the gospel being about personal salvation and escaping this terrible world for heaven. The good news is really about how heaven is coming to earth. When we talk about heaven, we're not talking about a geographical place way up in outer space but the unseen reality of God, which is actually all around us and within us. This reality, which is also called the kingdom, is going to come or be unveiled within all as righteousness, peace, and joy. This is part of the movement we must call youth to join.

> *Your kingdom come, your will be done, on earth as it is in heaven.*
> **– Matthew 6:10 (NIV)**

> *The kingdom of this world has become the kingdom of our Lord and of his Christ.*
> **– Revelation 14:11b (NASB)**

The "gospel of the kingdom" is supposed to create within us a vision towards peacemaking and the reconciliation of the world. It should create visionaries with the big picture in mind and hearts alive with purpose and love in their daily lives. The human being (that means you) is a temple of the Source and Life of the universe; and the Messiah who is the Alpha foundation of existence and who is leading existence to its Omega point of love is not over here or over there or reigning from Jerusalem—he reigns from within you.

So, back to the coffee shop where I was sitting with this teen—the one who's been coming to our youth group—and it turns out he's been enjoying what he's experiencing. He's becoming more and more intrigued by what he's been hearing. He looked at me and he said, "Brock, I've never heard the stuff you guys have been talking about before I came to the youth group. It's like you have this incredible hope for the world."

First of all, I was a bit shocked that a teen was being so articulate and had just been soaking it all in like this. (Of course, he was going to go to William and Mary on a full academic scholarship, but still.) He was understanding what the gospel was really about. He was light-years ahead of most of us. He didn't mention hell or how we get to go to heaven; he was, in his own words, wondering about how to be a part of bringing light and love and hope here on earth. This was the perfect moment to invite him into the cause.

4. EVANGELISM THEN MUST RELY ON THE HOLY SPIRIT TO DO THE CONVINCING, NOT APOLOGETICS.

As I've mentioned, when I was a boy everyone went to church every Sunday morning and Sunday night. Honestly, it was torture. But the best part of Sunday evenings was when church was over. We'd head out for pizza to hang, play Galaga, and watch ABC's Sunday night movie. It was a ball. But one Sunday evening we walked into the pizza parlor and there were three men arguing at one of the tables. I recognized two of them from church, but the third guy I had never seen. The argument was getting heated and loud, and the two men from our church were yelling at the third guy. So, I pulled on my dad's sleeve and asked what was happening. He told me the two guys from our church were trying to convince the other guy, who was Jewish, that Jesus really was the Messiah. Right then and there I knew that probably wasn't the best tactic for evangelizing.

So, let's go back again to the teen in the coffee shop. I was sitting there amazed by what God had been doing in his life. I couldn't believe how the conversation was going and how we had gotten there. God had brought him to our youth group, he somehow had become wide open to Jesus—which was a miracle in and of itself—and we were sitting there together… and I was just praying under my breath.

I couldn't help but thank God for what he was doing by the Holy Spirit in this boy's life. See, he was never argued into the kingdom, no one ever is. And we know this because as good Christians we've memorized the book of Ephesians, which tells us that the gospel is God-initiated, God-carried-out, and

God-fulfilled. None of us can boast.

Which, again, is why I love Alpha Youth. You can watch teens come in with their minds already made up that they don't believe in this nonsense; but by the end, almost across the board, everyone has opened their lives to Christ. It kills me every time. It's just an eight- to twelve-week conversation around a table after a meal once a week. We just ask questions and somehow the Holy Spirit works through these questions. I'm blown away every time I see it. There's no preaching, no altar call, none of that.

I think one of the main reasons why evangelism has gotten a bad rap is because of poor theology. Somewhere along the way we stopped trusting that God actually is the One who saves, that he draws us to himself—he's the One who is working. All we have to do is partner with what he's already doing.

So, I got to watch this teen not only slowly coming to faith, slowly waking up to the things of God, but also becoming a light. We left that coffee shop, and he was a changed person. Literally.

And that is today's evangelism. It's evolution: a slow subtle process of God moving by his Holy Spirit, revealing the good news of Jesus.

It's not "one and done." It's not "hit it and quit it."

It's not knocking on someone's door or yelling out at a Nationals baseball game and then walking away. It's not a presentation; it's life. Humble living. It's joining the world, not running from it.

And I think a good question for us to end this point on is this: *Does an unbelieving youth's encounter with you and your team*

5. EVANGELISM SHOULD BE AN ANNOUNCEMENT OF GOOD NEWS NOT NEWS LACED IN FEAR.

My wife was pinned down by her older brother when they were children, demanding that she believe in Jesus, so she wouldn't go to hell. She refused. But ultimately, when she was a teenager, the love and hope of the good news convinced her.

Even today she will say that the fear of hell was never an impetus for her to follow after God and to love Jesus. The transformative love of God is what won her.

If your gospel is not at least making *some* people feel like it's a license to sin, then it's probably not the gospel. The early apostles' preaching of the gospel resulted in people thinking it was a license to sin, which is why they had to address that it wasn't, that we shouldn't sin just because grace abounds, and that the grace of God teaches us to say no to ungodliness. This is a necessary clarification if you do see people thinking the outlandish love and grace revealed in Christ is a license to sin. But the apostles had to address it because the gospel they were preaching sometimes made people think it.

A gospel laced in fear is not the gospel at all, and it doesn't even resonate with today's teenagers. A recent study showed why young people are walking away from the church. The number one reason was that churches seem overprotective and full of fear.[12]

A few of the defining characteristics of today's teens and young adults are their unprecedented access to other ideas and the worldviews, as well as their prodigious consumption of popular culture. Christian teens are expressing the desire for their faith

189

in Christ to connect to the world they live in. However, much of their experience of Christianity feels stifling, fear-based, and risk-averse.

One quarter of eighteen- to twenty-nine-year-olds said, "Christians demonize everything outside of the church." Other perceptions in this category include the church "ignoring the problems of the real world" and even "my church is too concerned that movies, music, and video games are harmful" (18%).[13]

What is winning youth over today is a return to the gospel. What's winning youth today is actually good news for their families, their neighborhoods, and their world.

6. EVANGELISM SHOULD BE ALL HUMILITY.

Recently I was having dinner with a few guys who are in seminary here in the DC area. They're all very smart and funny, but extremely sarcastic with a touch of arrogance. I really like them, and I'm annoyed by them at the same time.

At dinner they were laughing and making fun of a local church here in the area, which is growing like crazy and whose theology is more on the lite side of charismatic. Now I would not call myself charismatic; I'm a bit of a theological mutt. But as I've explained, I do embrace the Holy Spirit—as I think every Christian should.

But one of these guys made this statement: "You'd have to be an idiot to go to that church."

The funny thing was—and they didn't know this—I had been attending that church for the better part of a year before I was hired at our current church. I tried to get a word in edgewise and bring a bit of perspective, but to no avail. Their seminary was teaching them that other perspectives and theological frameworks don't matter and have no legitimacy. What we're talking about is zero humility. (I can't even imagine what their interactions with people outside of the faith are like if they can't humbly acknowledge differing theological perspectives within the faith.)

So, I want to take you back to that coffee shop and the young man one last time. See, as I was sitting there with him in Starbucks, my goal was not to convince him my way of thinking was the right way or my theology was the correct one. I also didn't come to the table thinking I knew more than he did. A good evangelist in a post-Christian world understands that they're co-learners. This is appealing to the world—humble, curious, fun, inquisitive Christians.

And while we were sitting there, he said, "Brock, I just don't know if I can become a Christian, because it would kill my family. And then I'm also afraid of what I'm getting myself into. Will I have to be like all of these crazy Christians who are on *Fox and Friends*?"

I looked at him and said, "Yes, definitely you'll need to be like the people on *Fox and Friends*." We both laughed—probably too hard. But again, no one was trying to convince anyone of anything here. I trust God in this teen's life and my goal is to stay humble and curious and enjoy what the Holy Spirit is doing.

See, youth like this teen need to be let off the hook. They need to know it's okay to have a differing opinion—to journey and explore a bit before landing.

They need to know that Christians have all kinds of perspectives and viewpoints on a host of issues, and it's okay. In fact, it's beautiful that the faith is broad and there's enough room for all of us. Youth today need to see how big our orthodoxy is. That there is room for them and where they're at in their current understanding.

I remember when I first started out in ministry—fresh out of studying theology in school for about eight years and completely full of my own knowledge and understanding of the Scriptures. It's funny to think about how arrogant and sure I was. But what's even more funny is that the older I get and the more experience I have, the less I seem to know. Am I getting more ignorant or is there a beautiful humility that comes with age? I'm hoping for the later. Humility is an attractive quality, and it's also just plain honest. And the best at this are the Millennials.

LEARNING FROM THE YOUNG

So much is being said today about teens and Millennials walking away from the faith, and much is being said about reaching them. But the funny thing, actually, is that young people are beating all other generations in evangelism. It just looks different. I mean we see young people truly living *out* the good news through their social activism and hearts for the poor and for justice. But new research is telling us they also defy expectations as the generation that practices evangelism the most.

In fact, in answer to the question of evangelism being on the rise or in decline, it is the Millennials who are a rare case. While the evangelistic practices of all other generations have either declined or remained static in the past few years, Millennials are the only generation among whom evangelism is significantly on the rise. Their faith-sharing practices have escalated from 56% in 2010 to 65% in 2013.[14]

Not only that, but born-again Millennials share their faith more than any other generation today. Nearly two-thirds (65%) have presented the gospel to another person within the past

192

year, in contrast to the national average of about half (52%) of born-again Christians.[15]

But what is important to note is that the research tells us they're evangelizing differently than the old-fashioned crusades, youth rallies, and (my favorite) tent meetings. They're doing it through story, humility, and allowing people to journey and process and land in different theological places. They're simply keeping Jesus the focus. For them, relationship is king. They allow the sharing of ideas, they let people into their lives, they focus on community (belonging before believing, "I don't reject you because you're gay"), and they pursue meaningful relationships.

Maybe instead of talking about how Millennials take too many selfies, we should be applauding how they're the only ones actually reaching a post-Christian world in significant ways.

So, here are some questions to ponder:

- Do we really believe the good news is for the here and now, not just for the life after death?
- What is good news for today's pluralistic world?
- Do Christian have a message of good news for our sexuality? (Besides "stop touching that," which isn't really good news at all.)
- What is the good news for people who are resonating with Buddhism?
- With an epidemic of anxiety riddled people, especially teens, what is good news for them?
- What is the good news for people who just can't make the leap to faith because of intellectual or scientific reasons?
- Does the good news first come by way of deep-spirited friendship?[16]

You've climbed too many mountains and crossed too many rivers to stop and turn back now.
— Eleanor Brownn
Mile 9

CHAPTER 14
ENTREPRENEURIAL YOUTH WORKERS
AND THE NEED FOR LONGEVITY

My first full-time job as a youth worker was at a Presbyterian church in the Los Angeles area. I was the director of the seventh and eighth grade and I couldn't have been more excited. I had just gotten married, and we were so stoked to begin this new adventure. I was making the amazing amount of $25,000 per year. Now, even for the 90s this was barely above the poverty level, especially for Los Angeles; so we were constantly trying to figure out how to make ends meet. We managed apartment buildings, took side jobs, and basically tried to live with an extremely low overhead. I was also told that if I grew the youth group and proved my worth, then maybe they could figure out how to get me an increase in my salary. I wasn't sure what that meant in terms of actual dollars, but it was motivating for a young twenty-three-year-old.

So, we went to work to grow that youth group. We started that first summer with about ten junior highers, but by September of that fall we had launched an after-school program that brought in a bunch more. And by October, we had a few hundred seventh and eighth graders coming every Wednesday night. It was amazing, and it also meant massive work. But hey, we loved it and we were young, naive, and just amazed by what God was doing.

After about nine months of working there I remember sitting in an all-church business meeting. Now Presbyterians have a congregational form of government, so that means everything is known budget-wise and everything has to get approved by the whole congregation. So, they put everyone's salaries on the big screen in front of the whole church, and I noticed a couple of things right away. First, I had one of the lowest salaries. Part-time people were making what I was making. Secondly, they were trying to hire a small groups director for the church and they needed approval for this person's salary, which would be a whopping $95,000. (I was shocked. I thought maybe I should be applying for that small groups director position.)

But I knew my review was coming up, so I thought, "Well, I couldn't have worked any harder, and I couldn't have grown the group any bigger. I should be getting a pretty hefty raise." Or so I thought. I remember walking into the review with the head pastor and the executive pastor; I was excited and a bit nervous.

They began by affirming my socks off. Which felt pretty awesome for a young minister. They told me I had exceeded every expectation they'd had, that I was a great addition to the staff, and that I was delightful to work with. Okay, so I'm not sure about the delightful part, but everything they told me made me feel really good. Then it came. They paused and said, "We just want to honor your hard work and give you a raise."

"Yes!" said my inner voice.

They continued, "So, we're giving you a $500 raise."

I asked, "Five hundred dollars a month?"

"No," they responded. "That's $500 per year."

"Oh…"

I walked out confused. I was happy they were happy with the ministry I'd been doing, but the more I thought about it the more I realized I would never be valued there and that youth ministry as a whole was obviously not on the list of high-level investments for the church.

A LITTLE BACKGROUND

So, what happens as youth workers is we just get tired of struggling financially. Then add on the desire to have a position that has church-wide influence. This systemic problem begins to cause many of us to think of what else we might do. We've got this heavy calling on our lives, but it just doesn't seem doable long term. It's a frustration almost every youth worker goes through unless he or she is the main youth pastor at a mega-church.

Now I realize that for the most part around the country things have gotten a lot better, but I still see it. There is a mentality that youth ministry positions are still entry-level positions. That it's a training ground position or a stepping stone that will set you up for bigger and better and more important things. This has kept the paycheck low and the respect level low.

So, what I'd like to do now is to make an argument for the longevity of youth ministry but then talk about some practical ways to make that happen.

As I'm sure you may know, historically, youth ministry wasn't even a legitimate career path at all. In fact, for the most part, churches didn't really have paid youth workers until the late 1970s. But after churches saw the success of Youth for Christ (YFC), Fellowship of Christian Athletes (FCA), Young Life, and others in the 1960s, they wanted their own clubs and youth rallies. They were liking what they were seeing, and so they offered positions to parachurch people to come work for them. These awesome volunteer youth workers thought, "You mean you'll pay me to do this?" and off they went. Of course, they'd also have to be the janitor (this is still a thing in the church today all over the country by the way), but hey, they were getting paid to do what they loved—minus the mopping of bathroom floors.

This began the professionalization of youth ministry, but it didn't at all make it a legitimate career option. What it did do was create a construct and a system of training for the someday "real" pastors, who would get their training in the children's and youth departments with the promise that, one day, they might be ready to take on their own congregations. This is the stepping-stone training model that is still alive today and that many churches still espouse.

In fact, I remember getting the opportunity to speak in the main service as a young youth worker in Southern California. I relished the opportunity and I gave it my all. Afterwards people were very complimentary and affirmed the message I gave, but I'll never forget when a woman asked me, "Brock, you did an amazing job this morning, so when are you going to become a 'real' pastor?"

Later that day, we were having a youth leaders' meeting at our home; and one of our volunteers, who was a history teacher at one of the middle schools in the area, was there. I asked him if anyone had ever asked him when he was going to become a principal. He smirked and said, "Why in the world would I want to be a principal? I'm a teacher, I love history, and I love the day-to-day grind of working with middle schoolers."

That conversation happened twenty years ago, and this volunteer leader is still teaching middle school history. Has he failed? Is he underachieving? Has he not become a "real" educator? How could he make a career of this when the natural—or might I say the "legitimate" progression—is to use teaching as a stepping stone to move up the ladder to becoming a headmaster?

Well, this is ridiculous, right? Of course it is—teaching as a career is not only honorable, it's also the norm. A progression up some invisible educators' ladder *isn't* typical. And yet youth pastors are expected to outgrow teaching youth and working with youth. Why? Because staying in youth ministry is still not the norm, even though many of us have given our lives and our careers to bringing legitimacy to the profession. Which is sad, because the richest years of youth ministry often happen only after decades of work.

I remember getting in an online argument (so lame) over whether or not older youth workers were better at youth ministry than younger youth workers. I'm still not sure how I stumbled into that ridiculous exchange, but there I was, giving my two cents. The funny thing is that it got a little heated. (Not from my end, of course…) But my point during the discussion was this: When you're first in youth ministry, your audience is pretty narrow—you have the ear of teenagers but not many others. You get a little older, maybe get married and have a child, and then suddenly college students and young adults are listening to you. You live life a bit more, raise your children, and suddenly parents are leaning in, taking notes. The problem with the stepping-stone concept is that just when parents start listening, many youth workers get out of youth ministry and move on—or just quit ministry altogether. For me it's a shame because they finally have the ear of both youth and parents.

My heroes have always been sixty-something-year-old youth workers. Teens listen to them because they know that they love them and have wisdom and knowledge to give them. But parents are listening because these veterans have raised kids and have so much to offer in the way of firsthand experience. At that point, a beautiful partnership is established. Parent and youth worker working together in a way that only a veteran can fully understand. But unfortunately, this isn't the case in most settings around the country. I even know churches who have fired youth workers based on their seasoned age. (Ugh.)

And when you think about it, embracing the stepping-stone model is basically affirming the belief that youth ministry is like a starter home that needs just a little TLC, so it can be resold for a profit. If this is the continuing attitude, then our teens get a miserable youth worker—or, at the very least, a dissatisfied one who longs for the head pastor position and ultimately does not feel called to the youth themselves.

The youth worker who is longing for a position further up the food chain finds herself detached from her assignment or at least never content in her role. Personally, I couldn't resell a starter home unless I kept it at an emotional distance and did not put any of my time and effort into making it my dream home. I would be saving that investment for later, for my "real" home. So, we shouldn't be surprised when the result of the starter-home, stepping-stone mindset is dissatisfied and un-invested youth workers; and a dissatisfied, un-invested youth worker is not a good youth worker at all.

One thing to know is that I'm not speaking without some experience here. I've taken a shot at hiring people who knew they weren't ultimately called to youth ministry. Honestly, this hasn't gone well for me. Youth ministry is really difficult, it's not for the thin-skinned or for those who wish they were somewhere else. When I've made those hires in the past, it was like pulling teeth to get them to do the consistent, everyday, in-the-trench grind of youth work. I was constantly having to motivate, constantly riding them to get up and get out there. The adolescent journey is such a roller-coaster ride—one day a teenager loves Jesus and then the next she is a Buddhist, hooking up with a stranger on Saturday night. It's not for the faint of heart. Calling is important.

In fact, it's everything.

But how can we be true to our calling when we are barely

making a living wage? I remember consulting with a church not long ago. They were looking to hire their next youth pastor, and so I asked them what the salary was. They said that they try to keep it right at a first-year teaching salary. Now, in most churches around the country this is basically the norm. The problem though is that teachers get raises. They get a masters degree and then get a huge bump in pay—eventually they even receive tenure. But many churches around the country keep the salary right there, around a first-year teacher's pay (or worse)—often with lesser benefits than the other pastors on staff. (It's very difficult to stay in it long term when the small groups director is making three times as much as you.)

The funny thing was that this church I was consulting with wanted a youth pastor with at least ten years' experience, yet they wanted to pay the person a first-year teacher's rate. (Maybe we should get summer vacation off, huh?)

CHANGING THINGS FROM WITHIN THE SYSTEM

I think ultimately why I struggle with the argument that youth ministry is for the young and that it's a training ground for real pastoring is because it's arguing from a place of power—it's an argument that supports the current and constant system that we live in: a hierarchal, archaic system.

For example, just this month a friend of mine, who is the youth pastor at a church that is a multi-site church, has been approached to go and oversee one of their other sites. He's doing such a bang-up job with the youth ministry that he's being recruited to leave youth ministry and go and oversee one of these video venues, which is perceived by the church as a step up, an advancement—a better opportunity within the church hierarchy. This is the mindset. Youth ministry is a stepping stone. Only in this case, it's a stepping stone to a situation that I believe actually has less impact, less teaching opportunity, and is away from his calling.

I take pride in living and arguing from the other side, advocating for longevity in youth work. I've been in youth ministry for over twenty-seven years, and I can tell you it has not been easy to stay. Mostly it is because of the systemic issues we're touching on here.

But ultimately, what I believe is that if we are going to see a movement, and it begins with the young, then we'll need as much experience in youth ministry as possible. Longevity matters. It matters to the mindset and to the richness of the work.

So, if you believe that like I do and you're in this for the long haul, how do we do it when—for the most part—our churches aren't paying us enough to raise a family on?

Here's where entrepreneurship comes in.

———————

I was talking with a couple of long-term youth pastors recently. One is about fifty and the other is almost sixty years old. (I'm in my forties trying to stay in the game.) And we're sitting there having coffee, and all I can think about is "How in the world have they done it?" They both have had kids go through college, they both have decent homes, and both seem to be doing alright. So, I asked them, "How do you make ends meet? How have you survived on a youth pastor's salary all of these years?"

They both laughed like they had some evil secret. They smirked at each other, and one of them said, "Businesses, bro."

Even though I am from Southern California, I was a little

204

annoyed with the "bro" part; but I think mostly I was annoyed they hadn't helped a brother out earlier. They went on to tell me that they have started side businesses and that these businesses have liberated them financially and set them free from stress. Because of that, they've been able to stay in youth ministry long term. They haven't had to rethink their careers because of a paycheck.

One of them flips homes with his wife, the other one has a couple of smaller businesses that bring in over $100,000 a year for his family. I was blown away.

I was speaking at a Nazarene camp in Oklahoma last summer. The guy who picked me up was one of the youth pastors who was putting the whole week together. As we drove the two hours to the campsite, I asked him what his plans were long term.

Now let me pause here, because I don't want to just quickly tell this story without you understanding the feel in the car. God's presence was thick, and when he went to answer this question, it felt inspired.

He said, "Brock I have really been sensing that God is going to be bringing a movement to the United States and the world through the youth culture over the next ten to fifteen years. The rate at which we're declining as a culture and the way God has worked throughout history, I'm just sensing God's heart in this whole thing." Then he said, "I just don't want to miss any of it." He went on to tell me that in order to stay in youth ministry for the long haul he started a t-shirt company that provides t-shirts to Oklahoma churches. He said it barely takes much of his time and he makes an additional $50,000 a year for his family.

I spoke that week and saw God do amazing things. But I came

home telling my wife about this youth pastor doing everything he could to be there in ministry—doing everything he could so that he could help usher in a new movement among youth. I just really believe God is longing to fill you with creativity and cause you to begin dreaming about sustainability.

Now, of course, there are more aspects to having sustainability in ministry than just the money. Obviously we have to be healthy, sexually pure, in a right working environment, grow in our church-wide and community-wide influence. But as I listen to youth workers around the country, I find that being able to make ends meet plays a huge role in longevity.

Overcoming this challenge might simply mean you run a business and volunteer in youth ministry, like my friend Bob. We call him our full-time volunteer. He's done everything he can to invest in the next generation as a lay person.

But whatever the key to your personal longevity is, I believe God has his hand on this generation's youth workers. Because in order to usher in his dream, it's going to take savvy, humble, in-it-for-the-long-haul kind of dreamers.

Only once in a thousand years or so do we get to hear a Mozart or see a Picasso or read a Shakespeare. Ali was one of them, and yet at his heart, he was still a kid from Louisville who ran with the gods and walked with the crippled and smiled at the foolishness of it all.

– Billy Crystal
Eulogy for Muhammad Ali, June 10, 2016

CHAPTER 15
THIS FOOLISH CALLING

I see it. I'm not sure if you do, but I've been seeing it a lot recently. Sure, we can moan, grumble, and complain all day about what's wrong with the church and with Christians and how small-minded we've become. But I've been seeing something different lately. Yes, it's below the surface, and you'll definitely miss it if you're not in the right place at the right time with the right people.

My wife works with the National Network of Youth Ministries (NNYM), and she and I both see youth workers all over the country who are not settling for status quo thinking or ministry. A movement is in the air, and a bunch of us are ready for the new, the fresh, the innovation that only God can bring to a world like the one we live in. But I'm definitely seeing it.

Jesus' followers are breathing new life into a movement. Enough of focusing on what was, or what if, or what is, but these people are thinking in terms of how things ought to be, and they're actually doing something about it. They sense this deep call that's moving them up out of the norm.

This is you and me. With grace in our hands and the gospel as our calling, we are living redemptive, restorative lives to change the world with confidence in partnership with all of creation that has been groaning for a long time for us to live awake and wide open.

I remember hearing Mike Yaconelli speaking at NYWC many years ago. Each year thousands of youth workers would gather and get receive a fresh vision for the coming twelve months. He spoke to us with such passion and he spoke to the deeper parts of each of us, calling us out of the norm and the status quo. As we listened, we weren't sure if we should laugh or cry, so we did both. We were a room full of youth workers with a twinkle in our eyes, who didn't quite fit in other departments in the church; but every one of us was longing for God to bring a renewal across the land. And our prayers were that it would start with our youth, who were dying for a life worth living. Wow, do I miss him.

I love the mischief and mild anarchy of April Fools' Day. All the children who swap sugar for salt and the teenagers making their own fake news for fun. In 270 AD, an orphaned teenager called Anthony did something even more crazy. He foolishly walked away from the wealth he'd inherited. Entrusting his younger sister to "a group of virgins," he camped out alone in the wilderness for fifteen years. During this time, he grew an amazing beard and prayed constantly. It was an absurd kind of rebellion, but it changed the world. And it all began when he was eighteen years old and his parents both died.

The suffering caused him to long for more, and he was willing to do anything, even if it looked like insanity. He decided to follow the evangelical counsel of Jesus whose motto was, "If you want to be perfect, go, sell what you have and give to the poor, and you will have treasure in heaven" (Matthew 19:21, NKJV). So, Anthony gave away some of his family's lands to his neighbors, sold the remaining property, and donated all of the money to the poor. Anthony "of the Desert" (as he became known) foresaw a time when sanctity would resemble insanity. (Sounds like middle school ministry, huh?)

But legend tells us that Satan went after Anthony and fought him there in the desert like he did with Jesus. The devil afflicted him with boredom, laziness, and he was plagued with a strong lust for women. So, Anthony did what any of us would do. He succumbed to the temptation by getting online and looking at naughty pictures behind closed doors.

No. Not at all.

He overcame all this temptation by praying. He prayed powerful prayers and discovered God in a freeing kind of way. A liberation came over him and he emerged from his pilgrimage in the desert ready to give to the next generation. For the remainder of his years he invested in the young, pouring everything God had given him to equip them for the renewal that the world was longing for.

He once said, "A time is coming when men will go mad, and when they see someone who is not mad, they will attack him, saying, 'You are mad; you are not like us.'"[17]

I have felt that way in elder meetings.

But the point is clear, the day to be foolish is not just April Fools' Day. God is calling us to have faith like his little ones—naïve, bold, and faith-filled children. He's calling us to barrel loads of laughter; to play tricks and maybe some '70s disco music; but, most of all, to play the holy fool. He's calling us to dream again.

BIG FOOLISH DREAMS

In the spring of 2015, my wife, daughter, and I all had a dream. We felt like God was calling us to start a nonprofit to help develop next-generation leaders who would instigate change for the common good. We were on a prayer walk one night, and all of us at the same time got a sense that God wanted us to move to Washington DC. Why? We didn't know, but after a few more confirmations we loaded up our truck and headed to Tennessee.

Huh?

Yeah, we had no money or a place to live in Washington DC, so we shacked up with my wife's parents and prayed that God would open doors for us in DC. But before I tell you what happened, I first have to tell you that on that prayer walk, when we felt like God said DC, we also got a sense that he wanted us to be in Washington DC by September 1. I know this sounds weird and a bit foolish, but hang with me for a moment.

We went to Tennessee to the in-laws' home (they are awesome, by the way), and we were just waiting. Waiting for a door to open. Waiting for something to happen. Just waiting for God to do something, anything. June went by. July went by. August was almost gone, and I was beginning to freak out a bit. Like, "God, I thought you said DC by September 1? What's going on?"

Well, one day I was walking outside there in Dayton, Tennessee; and it felt like 120 degrees out with 100% humidity. So, at the moment, I wasn't sure if it was the heat or if it was divine. But a man's name popped in my head: Jeff Puryear. He was an old friend of my dad's, who I thought might still live in the DC area. And I couldn't get his name out of my head, so I called my dad up and told him. My dad said, "Wow, Jeff has been on my mind all day long. I should call him." (Ya think?)

Well my dad gave him a call and, indeed, he still lived in DC. My dad told him we were launching a new initiative, a nonprofit called Generation514, and that we were looking for free housing. Jeff said, "That's funny. I have a rental that I can't seem to find a renter for, which is highly unusual. Your son and his family can stay there for as long as they want for free, and it's available September 1st." We pulled into the driveway of that home on the afternoon of September 1. God is good. I'm serious, he's so good!

In fact, I had a friend tell me once that if you're ever doubting that God works, just look for the coincidences. Eventually there will be so many you'll start to think maybe they're not mere coincidences.

It's all just foolishness, isn't it? God is looking for a little foolishness, I think.

A young guy in England named Pete Greig was talking with some of his friends, and they discovered together that not one of them really knew how to pray. So, they decided to pray for twenty-four straight hours in a little prayer room they put together. The United Kingdom had been post-Christian at this time for over fifty years, and many hadn't seen hide nor hair of God in those years. In fact, I had heard throughout the '90s that it would take an act of the Divine himself for anything of substance to actually happen there.

But nonetheless Pete and his friends prayed that twenty-four hours and haven't stopped praying for over eighteen years now. They started inviting young people into the prayer space, and something remarkable happened. Youth actually started coming, and coming in droves, and it has spread like wildfire. Since then over 10,000 such prayer rooms have emerged around the globe and are in over half of the world's countries. Over two million youth have encountered the risen Jesus in these spaces, and this whole time they have never stopped praying—night and day, nonstop, 24/7.

People told Pete and his friends that this was the most ridiculous way to reach today's young people. But God's Spirit beckoned them onward. And what seemed like foolishness, God used and is using powerfully right now as we speak.

A few years later, another youth worker in England by the name of Mike Pilavachi had a different dream. His dream was to have a summer youth camp for the struggling teenagers in Europe. Everyone told him that post-Christian youth there would never go to a Christian camp. But after years of dreaming, scheming, and praying, he went forward with the camp. Thousands came and thousands found Jesus. They've been doing this camp for years now and have seen hundreds of thousands of youth give their lives to whatever Jesus is calling them to do in the world. But it all just seemed so foolish at the time.

A youth pastor in New England decided he wanted to reach the post-Christian teens there, and after trying everything from fun game nights to pizza feeds, he finally went away in discouragement to pray and hopefully discover why God would even bring him and his family to a place like this. But in that prayer time he got an idea. What if he just showed these teens that the most spiritual life they could ever have was one that was wide open to Jesus? So, he started having prayer nights, times of healing prayer, and tried to create sanctuary for these stressed out teens.

Everyone thought he was crazy. The local Young Life leader told him it would never work. But God showed up, teens actually started inviting their friends, and a little movement was born.

Maybe God is calling us to be foolish, to dream again, and to dare to engage with this new adventure?

A friend of mine in Ohio had an idea that youth ministry really needed to be about developing youth. Teens weren't coming out to youth group anymore in his church, but they sure were involved in their schools' sports programs, plays, and music departments. Like me and many other youth workers around the country, he wondered if students were so committed to it all because they owned it. He wondered if the reason why

214

they never missed even a practice was because they saw that they were needed and had a role to play. So, he met with a few of them who were ready to lead. He'd invested in them and mentored them, giving them the vision that faith isn't just something to believe in but something to actually do. So, together with this youth pastor, these teens began praying over what God might do. They planned the talks, put together worship teams, had this youth pastor teach them how to pray for their friends, and then they invited the community in. And of course you know what happened, the youth group exploded.

Here's the funny yet terribly tragic thing: This youth pastor lost his job. His pastor wanted a traditional youth ministry; and so he fired my friend, hired a different kind of youth worker, and now the group has shrunk to nothing again. (I'm not really sure what's foolish in this case.)

It's easy to read a chapter like this and not realize what a calling to young people really looks like today, that there's tremendous sacrifice. But I have a feeling you're just the type God is longing to use.

WHY YOU?

I love going to youth worker conferences. There's nothing like being in a room full of youth workers. Nothing. The great thing about youth workers is that we're all a bit strange, odd, different; we've been destroyed by Jesus and awakened to the heartbeat of God for the next generation. (Plus, the idea of leading adult Sunday school makes us all throw up a little bit in our mouths.)

I did mention that I came from a long line of pastors (three generations); but, to be more specific, I come from a long line of youth workers—you know, those underpaid, overworked, weirdoes who still have a twinkle in their eyes, who refuse to grow all the way up. I am, in fact, a fourth-generation youth worker.

My great grandmother was the first youth worker in my family. She led the youth in her church from the 1920s through the 1940s. All the teens in the church would fight to sit next to her during the Sunday morning services.

One day a young twelve-year-old little girl walked into the church. Her father owned the local pub in the area, and this little girl just felt lost in the midst of all the dysfunction in her home. But something, or Someone, compelled her to come to church that morning. Immediately my great grandmother noticed her. (It's funny how great youth workers have this built-in radar that helps them notice when a young person walks in the room.) So, my great grandmother walked over to this this twelve-year-old girl and asked if she wanted to sit with her and some other kids during church. At the end of the service, the pastor gave an altar call; but this little girl didn't move. Instead, directly after the service, she asked my grandmother what it meant to invite Jesus into her heart. So Great Grandma told her all about it and then asked her if she'd like to ask Jesus to be her Lord and Savior. The little girl prayed and her life was never the same.

In fact, this little girl—a few years later—ended up marrying my great grandmother's son. She became my grandmother, and she and my grandfather also invested in young people. Every summer they would run camps for young people all over the state of Oregon. And then many years later on the scene came my hero, my father. He was such a great youth worker that I felt like I needed to carve my own trail and not go into youth ministry at all. But God had a completely different plan for me that was revealed to me by a mentor of mine my freshman year of college. Since then I've been pointing youth to Jesus every day.

But as you and I know, the church is not an easy place to work in and for, so sometimes we forget why we do this. We get caught in patterns and sometimes we end up doing things that don't necessarily work like they used to. So, God has to get our attention, make us desperate, and open us up to the possibility of something that initially might sound like foolishness. But the reality is that the world is desperate for youth workers to enter into the culture—fully alive, filled with the Spirit, and with a full understanding of who they are and what they're called to.

So, here's the truth…

TRUTH #1: YOU HAVE VISION FOR WHO TEENS ARE AND WHO THEY ARE BECOMING.

All we hear these days is how young people are going to hell in a handbasket. They're selfish, self-centered, and addicted. (Like previous generations didn't have their issues.) But here's the truth, God is calling you to be his eyes and vision for this next generation, giving perspective and hope to these kids who have been dismissed, thrown away, given up on. Many might be annoyed by them, but you see something in them that no one else can see. (Heck, the youth themselves don't even see it.) But God has given you his eyes.

And guess what? Someone probably did it for you too.

Or, maybe no one did this for you, and that's why you're in youth ministry now. Because you have to, you can't do anything else, and the reason is because you are *called* to carry this vision.

The reality is this: Youth ministry is something we didn't choose, it chose us. And it makes us weird, strange, and foolish. One day we woke up sitting across from some burrito-smelling middle schooler and we thought, "How on earth did I get here?"

Who else is spending their afternoons and evenings between three and ten meeting with teens because they're concerned about their emotional and spiritual well-being? No one!

Who in their right mind would give away every weekend to shuttle teenagers to retreats, sleep on the floor, give Harry his meds so he doesn't start bouncing off the walls, and call all that that kingdom work? You would, and you do it all because you and I both know this work is holy, it's divine. You have been hand-picked by God, and he's given you this transcendent vision to see what he's doing in and through these precious ones in your care.

TRUTH #2: YOU MAKE CHURCH THE SAFEST PLACE ON EARTH FOR YOUTH.

Your youth do not feel safe anywhere else; but with you they feel safe to screw up, safe to make mistakes, safe to doubt the faith, safe to confront their sexuality, safe to be at their worst. Why? Because that's what Jesus did for you and me—he destroyed us, he ruined us by his extravagant grace. We know the grace that has been extended to us, as broken as we are, and we're compelled to extend that same stuff to these amazing teens.

Let's face it, this generation goes to school and is filled with so much anxiety that they cannot face the thought of tomorrow. This generation doesn't feel safe—at home, at school, with their friends, anywhere. It's why, as Chap Clark has pointed out when he speaks on the topic, they have developed the art of living multiple authentic selves. As you read in chapter one, they just put on the safest self, according to whatever the environment happens to be that they're walking into. So, little Johnny might be one way in math class but a completely different person in science class. Why? The teacher is different, the room is different, the other students are different, and he is different because he just wants to feel some semblance of safety.

Not long ago we were in Jamaica with Praying Pelican Missions on a mission trip, and a teen and I were talking. Out of nowhere she took in a deep breath and said, "I haven't felt this safe in my entire life."

See this is what we do: The essence of youth ministry is creating environments where teens can experience the warmth of God, and you do this by your very presence. They run into you at the mall and they're reminded that they're safe. God's warmth travels everywhere you go. This is what you do and it's because of the way you live. Teens around you know that you not only love them but you actually like them—and this echoes God's very heart. You've discovered the heartbeat of God because the truth is you've run into the God who doesn't just love you but genuinely likes you. He enjoys you, just because you are who you are. See, he's particularly fond of you. And so you're filled with a desire to introduce these teens around you to the God who *likes*, and that, my friends, is revolutionary.

TRUTH #3: YOU ARE THE PROPHETIC VOICE FOR THE CHURCH TODAY.

The church has been turned into a bunch of businesses and well-oiled machines that the early followers of Jesus wouldn't even recognize today. But because you have taken on the role of the youth worker, you exist outside of that machine—and you speak for this generation. You're living out on the edges, doing whatever it takes to reach people with the good news of the gospel. I have never met a group of people more passionate about exploring the changing landscape of culture and relating that to the church. We are about the evaluating, critiquing, and upheaval of the old.

Which one of us doesn't have a sense that a spiritual revolution is just around the corner?

Some of us work in great churches and have authority and a voice for change, but most of us don't. When we speak in a staff meeting, they roll their eyes and pat us on our heads. Then they parade our youth on youth Sunday saying, "Look what we've done." And this breaks our hearts, because we love the church and we so long for them to get it and to have a genuine place for teens at the table. But they're missing it.

Now here's some truth though: God has given you insight into culture's trenches where it's complex and messy, and he has filled you with his Spirit, which enables you to see truth wherever it is. But this isn't in vain, God will give you favor to prophetically speak to the church, and you must.

SO, I LEAVE YOU WITH THIS...

You are not alone, and this town or city you work in is not full of youth ministry competitors. Every youth worker you have ever met or run into is family. We're a tribe of people who don't quite fit other places; and when we come into rooms full of youth workers, we don't need to explain ourselves. You belong to a group who will never ask you, "So what is it you do again when you're not in the office?" We get it. We aren't rivals—we are cohorts and collaborators bringing the kingdom to one of the darkest places on earth: youth culture. We belong to this calling and we belong to each other. You're not reading this book alone and you're not in this mission alone.

So, breathe deep. You're safe.

Safe to laugh.

220

Safe to vent.

Safe to be yourself.

We get it, you don't need to explain yourself.

See, God is calling us to the foolish, the daring, and the unconventional.

So, here's to the holy rascals. Here's to the mischief-makers and the revolutionaries. Here's to the ones called to usher in a new thing and call a generation out of darkness and into his marvelous light. Here's to those who find themselves laughing at the world's folly all day and weeping for it all night long. Here's to the ones whom God has so filled with hope that they see the future—the upside down, backwards kingdom future. The future where youth are leading the way.

Here's to you.

ENDNOTES

1. Al Aronowitz, "Chapter 2: St. Jack," *The Blacklisted Journalist* (online), Column 22, June 1, 1997: http://www.blacklistedjournalist.com/column22.html.

2. "The Alternative Jesus: Psychedelic Christ," *Time Magazine*, Vol. 97, No. 25, "The Jesus Revolution," June 21, 1971.

3. Lewis's inaugural lecture at Cambridge, November 29, 1954. C. S. Lewis, "De Descriptione Temporum," 9-25.

4. Anne Lamott, *Plan B: Further Thoughts on Faith* (New York: Riverhead, 2004).

5. Richard Dawkins, *River Out of Eden: A Darwinian View of Life* (New York: Basic Books, 1995).

6. Francis Chan, *Forgotten God: Reversing Our Tragic Neglect of the Holy Spirit* (Colorado Springs, Colo.: David C. Cook, 2009).

7. Thom and Joani Shultz, *Why Nobody Wants to Go to Church Anymore: And How 4 Acts of Love Will Make Your Church Irresistible* (Loveland, Colo.: Group, 2013).

8. For more from Tim, head to timothyeldred.com.

9. Ralph Winter, "The Two Structures of God's Redemptive Mission." *Perspectives on the World Christian Movement: A Reader*, eds. Steven Hawthorne and Ralph Winter (Pasadena, Calif.: William Carey Library, 2013).

10. Tolerance: Dictionary.com, *Dictionary.com Unabridged. Random House, Inc.*: http://www.dictionary.com/browse/tolerance (accessed: July 20, 2017).

11. Demographic Study, "America's Changing Religious Landscape," *Pew Forum* (online), May 12, 2015: http://www.pewforum.org/2015/05/12/americas-changing-religious-landscape/.

12. Releases in Millenials and Generations, "Six Reasons Young Christians Leave the Church," *Barna* (online), September 27, 2011: https://www.barna.com/research/six-reasons-young-christians-leave-church/.

13. Ibid.

14. Research Releases in Culture and Media, "Three Digital Life Trends for 2014," *Barna: FRAMES* (online), March 10, 2014: https://www.barna.org/barna-update/culture/657-three-digital-life-trends-for-2014.

15. Research Releases in Faith and Christianity, "Is Evangelism Going Out of Style?" *Barna* (online), December 17, 2013: https://www.barna.org/barna-update/faith-spirituality/648-is-evangelism-going-out-of-style.

16. Research Releases in Faith and Christianity, "Barna Studies the Research,

Offers a Year-in-Review Perspective," *Barna* (online), December 20, 2009: https://www.barna.org/barna-update/faith-spirituality/325-barna-studies-the-re search-offers-a-year-in-review-perspective.

17. Benedicta Ward, *The Sayings of the Desert Fathers: The Alphabetical Collection* (Collegeville, Minn.: Liturgical Press, 1984).